The Same Deep Water As Me

Nick Payne's *If There Is I Haven't Found It Yet* was
staged at the Bush Theatre in 2009 and went on to
receive that year's George Devine Award. He is a graduate
of the Young Writers' Programme at the Royal Court,
where his next play, *Wanderlust*, opened in 2010 and was
shortlisted for the *Evening Standard*'s Most Promising
Playwright Award. *One Day When We Were Young*,
in a Paines Plough and Sheffield Theatres production,
was staged at the Crucible Studio Theatre, Sheffield,
in 2011, and later transferred to Shoreditch Town Hall
as part of the Roundabout Season. *Constellations*, which
opened at the Royal Court in 2012 and transferred to the
Duke of York's Theatre, won the *Evening Standard*
Theatre Award for Best Play.

NICK PAYNE

The Same Deep Water As Me

faber and faber

First published in 2013
by Faber and Faber Ltd
74–77 Great Russell Street
London WC1B 3DA

Typeset by Country Setting, Kingsdown, Kent CT14 8ES
Printed in England by CPI Group (UK) Ltd, Croydon CR0 4YY

A CIP record for this book
is available from the British Library

978-0-571-31100-2

2 4 6 8 10 9 7 5 3 1

Acknowledgements

John Crowley, Damian Rourke and Josie Rourke.

Julie Aldred, Alastair Coomer, Monica Dolan, Amy Edgington, Peter Forbes, Joanna Griffin, Paul Higgins, Isabella Laughland, Nigel Lindsay, Daniel Mays, Kirstie Nicholls, the Pearson Playwrights' Scheme, Kris Roper, Harry Sharpe, Dave Smith, Niky Wardley, Marc Wootton and all of the staff at the Donmar Warehouse.

Ben Hall and Lily Williams at Curtis Brown, and John Buzzetti at WME.

Minna.

Mum.

'The Same Deep Water As Me' is the title of a song from the second, self-titled album of the band I Am Kloot. I highly recommend both the album and the song itself.

This text was correct at the time of going to press but will not reflect any changes made during later rehearsals.

The Same Deep Water As Me was first performed at
the Donmar Warehouse, London, on 1 August 2013.
The cast was as follows:

Andrew Eagleman Daniel Mays
Barry Patterson Nigel Lindsay
Kevin Needleman Marc Wootton
Anne Monica Dolan
Guy Peter Forbes
Terri Joanna Griffin
Jennifer Needleman Niky Wardley
Georgina Monica Dolan
Judge Jessup Peter Forbes
Isabella Reynolds Isabella Laughland
Attendant Joanna Griffin

Director John Crowley
Designer Scott Pask
Lighting Designer Peter Mumford
Sound Designer Christopher Shutt
Casting Director Alastair Coomer CDG

Anne and Georgina could be played the same actress.
Guy and Jessup could be played by the same actor.
Terri and Attendant could be played by the same actress.

Characters

Andrew Eagleman
thirties

Gilly Whitworth (voice only)

Barry Paterson
fifty-five

Kevin Needleman
thirties

Steve Beers (voice only)

Anne Gunn
forty

Guy Haines
forty

Terri
under twenty

Jennifer Needleman
thirties

Graham Eagleman (voice only)

Georgina Burns
forty

Isabella Reynolds
twenty-two

Judge Jessup
fifty

Attendant

THE SAME DEEP WATER AS ME

For Dad

One

Late summer. Scorpion Claims. An extremely warm day.
Andrew, seated at a desk, is transcribing an interview
from a Dictaphone on to a desktop computer. A reasonably
sized desk fan whirs away.

Gilly (*voice*) We'd just had him neutered.

Andrew (*voice*) Right.

Gilly It was his first time out of the house. We wanted to
take him somewhere he knew. Somewhere recognisable.
Somewhere we hoped he wouldn't feel, say, too
intimidated.

Andrew Of course.

Gilly He was in his element.

Andrew Great.

Gilly We'd never seen him move so fast. Eventually, of
course, fatigue starts to set in. You're wearing me out, I
said. I'm going to have to take a little break. He moaned,
of course. Panting, trying to charge off. I need to eat my
sandwiches, I said. I'd made the sandwiches in a bit of
hurry – It's funny what you remember, isn't it?

Andrew Mmm.

Gilly I'd completely forgotten to butter the bread. I
started feeding Harry the bread and at that point, at that
point almost exactly, I felt this enormous great *thud*.

At some point during the above, the desk fan stops
working. Andrew bangs the fan itself a couple of
times. Nothing. Andrew stops the Dictaphone.

Andrew inspects the fan. Shakes it. Nothing. He clambers beneath the desk to inspect the plug. After a moment, enter Barry. Barry carries a large brown cardboard box. Barry is extremely sweaty and out of breath. Beat. The underside of the box suddenly gives way and its contents – flyers – go everywhere.

Barry Fuck a duck.

Andrew emerges from underneath the desk.

Andrew Alright?

Barry Been to the printers.

Andrew Oh yeah.

Barry Yeah. Got the new flyers. Exhausted. Sweating like a fucking dyslexic on *Countdown*.

Andrew moves to Barry and the pair begin to gather up the flyers.

Andrew Did we ask for green?

Barry What's that?

Andrew They're green, 's that what we asked for?

Barry Colour of the scorpion.

Andrew Is it?

Barry 'Cording to Neil.

Andrew Neil?

Barry Did the flyers.

Andrew Reckons they're green?

Barry Well some of 'em have gotta be.

Andrew Right.

Barry Darwin and that.

Andrew It says 'tail'.

Barry What's that?

Andrew I thought we'd agreed it should say 'tale'?

Barry You've lost me.

Andrew As in L–E? I thought we'd said that it should say –

Barry I thought it was tail as in tail. As in 'the tail of the scorpion'.

Andrew That's what I'm saying.

Barry Right.

Andrew D'you see what I'm saying?

Barry No.

Andrew I thought we'd agreed that it should say 'tale' as in L–E. As in, 'Scorpion Claims. We'll find the sting in the tale'. It's a play on words. Tale as in story. 'We'll find the sting in the *tale*' as in 'we'll find the sting in the *story*'.

Barry inspects a flyer.

Barry Fuck's sake.

Andrew Don't worry about it.

Barry Thing is . . .

Andrew Go on.

Barry Pretty big order.

Andrew Go on.

Barry Neil said he'd do us a deal.

Andrew Bet he fucking did. How many?

Barry Ten.

Andrew Ten?

Barry Boxes.

Andrew How many's in a box?

Barry Thousand.

Andrew Barry, you tryin'a give me a fucking heart attack.

Barry Get ten per cent off. Order ten thousand, get ten per cent off. Shall I bin 'em?

Andrew Bin 'em?

Barry Take 'em down charity shop.

Andrew Fucking hell, Barry. No. We're not gonna bin 'em. And we're certainly not gonna give 'em to fucking Oxfam.

   Beat.

Fan's on the blink.

Barry What's that?

Andrew Fan. 'S fucked.

Barry Tried turning it on and off?

Andrew Nothing.

Barry 'Kin hell. Fucking roasting.

Andrew Might nip to Greggs, fancy anything?

Barry Already been. Thanks.

Andrew Sly fucker.

Barry Needed to rehydrate. Got you a Yum Yum somewhere.

   Barry checks his pockets.

Andrew How's Neve?

Barry Yeah, not bad. Says hello.

Andrew How's her eye?

Barry 'Parently 's not infectious any more.

Andrew That's a relief. D'you get anything else?

Barry Maybe.

Andrew Go on.

Barry Steak Bake.

Andrew Barry, you dark fucking horse. How was it?

Barry Yeah, magic t' be honest with ya.

Andrew moves to a desk, gathers his keys, etc.

Andrew Back in a bit.

Buzzer goes. Andrew and Barry freeze, as it were.

Hold the phone. You got anyone coming in?

Barry shakes his head. Buzzer goes.

Right. Shit. Look sharp, Barry.

*Andrew perhaps straightens his tie a little. He exits.
Buzzer goes again, slightly more sustained. Barry
moves to the desk fan. Barry tries pressing the fan's
various buttons. Nothing. Barry shakes the fan. Again
he tries the fan's various buttons. Nothing. He kneels
down and attempts to inspect the plug. Enter Andrew
and Kevin.*

Kevin Needleman, this is Barry Paterson. Barry specialises
in clinical negligence.

Kevin Hiya, Barry, alright.

Barry Hello, Kevin, good to meet ya.

Andrew Kevin and I were at school together.

Kevin He was a right little shit.

Barry Some things never change.

Andrew Not seen each other for years.

Kevin Gotta be ten, eleven, at least.

Barry Blimey.

Kevin Thought you was living in London?

Andrew I am. Was. Moving about.

Barry Walker fucking Texas Ranger.

Kevin 'Member Jordan saying you was in Arsenal?

Andrew There or thereabouts, yeah.

Kevin Bit of a trek? Arsenal to Luton.

Andrew Be surprised. So what can we –

Kevin The one that got away, eh?

Andrew So what can we do for ya, Kevin?

Kevin Doesn't hang around, does he?

Barry Can we get you something to drink, Kevin?

Kevin Love a cup of tea.

Barry What d'you fancy? There's organic Green; White with Pomegranate; Ginger and Lemongrass; Cranberry, Strawberry and Raspberry; Organic Rose, Chamomile and Lavender; Dragonfly Yellow or Japanese Popcorn.

Kevin Fucking hell.

Andrew Barry did a course.

Barry Cornwall.

Kevin I'll be honest with ya, Barry, I'm a bit out of m' depth here, mate.

Barry Popcorn?

Kevin Yeah, go on then, why not, fuck it.

Exit Barry.

Is that . . . 'S not . . . Barry as in . . .

Andrew Go on.

Kevin 'S not Barry as in linesman Barry, is it?

Andrew It is, yeah.

Kevin Fuck me, he's changed.

Andrew Has he?

Kevin 'Member his missus? Fuck me, she definitely woulda got it. How's she looking these days?

Andrew She uh . . . She passed on.

Kevin That is a fucking tragedy.

Beat.

Boulders reckoned he saw you, you know.

Andrew Oh yeah.

Kevin In Greggs, coupla weeks ago. Reckoned he saw you chatting to that bird behind the counter.

Andrew Neve.

Kevin I said to him, I said, you reckon you saw Andrew-fucking-Eagleman. I said, Boulders, I said, you need y' fucking head read, mate. Eagleman bolted years ago, I said. Might text him actually.

Kevin goes to get out his phone.

Andrew So what can we do for ya, Kevin?

Kevin Well. Bit embarrassing to be honest with ya. In an accident, coupla weeks ago. Tesco van. One of them little ones.

Andrew I'm sorry to hear that.

Kevin Yeah, thanks. Anyway, I was, was speaking to a mate of mine. Robin Hillson? Karate Robin? Sneezed that time and his eye came out? Anyway Karate was saying similar thing happened to him. And he was saying that he put in one of these claims. One of these no-win-no-fee set-ups.

Enter Barry with tea.

Barry Here we are.

Barry hands Kevin tea.

Here's to it.

Barry and Kevin sip their tea.

Kevin Fuck me.

Barry What d'ya reckon? Mixture of green tea and sweetened corn. Japanese rave about it.

Kevin Fucking speechless to be honest with ya, Barry. (*To Andrew.*) Are you not a-partaking in the tea?

Andrew I'm alright.

Kevin Fuckin' hell. That's me done for the day, that is.

Andrew Kevin was just asking about no-win-no-fee.

Kevin Tesco van pranged inta the back of us.

Barry Nightmare. Whatever happened to every little 'elps.

Kevin Was saying to Andrew, similar thing happened to a mate of mine.

Barry Right.

Kevin Reckoned he did the whole no-win-no-fee; ended up with, like, ten, twelve grand.

Barry Depends on how you wanna approach it.

Kevin How d'ya mean?

Andrew Were you travelling alone?

Kevin Wife and daughter.

Barry They alright?

Kevin Yes and no; bit o' this bit o' that.

Barry How about the car?

Kevin How d'ya mean?

Barry Much damage?

Kevin Yeah, fair bit of damage. Bumper, brake lights. Look, I'm gonna be honest: can't afford to pay anything up front, thass the thing.

Barry Right.

Kevin Thass why this no-win thing sounds like a good idea, d'ya know what I mean?

Andrew We do.

Kevin Only pay if we win, right?

Barry In effect.

Andrew If we pursue your claim on a no-win-no-fee basis, Kevin, if your claim is then successful, myself and Barry would simply expect to receive our standard fee. And then on top of our standard fee, we would also expect to receive what we call an uplift or success fee. This tends to be around twelve to fifteen per cent of the standard fee.

Barry But that's jumping the gun a little.

Kevin What happens if we get nothing?

Andrew Then I'm afraid we all walk away empty-handed.

Kevin Do we have to go to court?

Andrew These sorts of claims very rarely make it to trial, if at all. For the sake of argument, though, let's say we are, for instance, requested to attend a two-day trial –

Kevin I don't wanna do *A Few Good Men*.

Andrew Come again?

Kevin 'You can't handle the truth.'

Andrew Right, no. 'S nothing like that. Civil trials are really informal. No one's tryin'a catch anyone out.

Kevin So how does it work?

Andrew Well, if you would like us to pursue your claim, the first thing that we would do would be to take a statement from yourself.

Barry Then we'd bung that in the post to Tesco.

Andrew And then everyone crosses their fingers.

Kevin Thass it?

Barry More or less.

Kevin When d'you wanna do the statement?

Andrew We could do it now if you've –

Barry Bit snowed under at the moment actually, Kevin. But why don't we take y' number and then one of us'll give you a ring to sort out a consultation. How's that sound?

Kevin Great, yeah.

Andrew passes Kevin a small notepad and a pen.

Andrew Why don't you pop your details on there?

Kevin writes down his home and mobile telephone numbers. While Kevin is doing so, Andrew silently attempts to gesture/mouth to Barry, 'Why didn't you want to take his statement now?'

Kevin You read that alright?

Barry Thass perfect.

Andrew holds out a hand for shaking.

Andrew Been great to see you, Kevin.

Kevin Yeah, likewise.

Kevin turns to shake Barry's hand.

Barry.

Barry Cheers, Kevin.

Kevin You'll be in touch.

Andrew We'll be in touch.

Kevin quickly downs the remainder of his tea, gasps with delight –

Kevin God bless the fucking Japanese.

– and exits. Beat.

Andrew You alright?

Barry Never been better.

Andrew How come y' didn't fancy getting a statement –

Barry Got a lot on.

Andrew Like what?

Barry That fan's not gonna fix itself.

Andrew Right.

Andrew and Barry move to their desks. Beat.

Barry Not sure I trust him.

Andrew Seemed alright.

Barry Not sold.

Andrew How so?

Barry Convenient innit. Happened to a mate, then he gets bumped; not sold.

Andrew Hairy muff.

Andrew fiddles with the fan a little further. Barry watches as Andrew perhaps grows a little frustrated. Andrew stands.

Goin'a Greggs. I will say this though, Barry: as beggars, can we be choosers?

Barry Who says we're beggin?

Exit Andrew. Barry begins to open a letter. The fan suddenly whirs into life; Barry watches.

A week or so later. Scorpion Claims. Sunset. Another hot, balmy day. Kevin, seemingly a little drunk. After a moment, enter Andrew with a cup of coffee. Andrew hands coffee to Kevin. A telephone begins to ring. Andrew hits the speakerphone button.

Andrew Scorpion Claims, Andrew speaking.

Steve (*voice*) Yeah, hello, Andrew, it's Steve Beers.

Andrew Hello, Steve, how are you? Good to hear from you.

Steve I'm well, thanks. How are you?

Andrew Busy, Steve, I'll be honest with you. We are bu–*sy*.

Steve That's good.

Andrew Never too busy for you, though, Steve. What can we do for ya?

Steve Well. I just. I wanted to call because. In all honesty, I'm afraid I'm beginning to wonder whether a little cut, my little cut, is really worth all this fuss?

Beat.

Hello?

Andrew Yeah. Still here, Steve.

Steve I was talking to a friend of a friend recently –

Andrew Right.

Steve He's a solicitor –

Andrew Steve, can I be honest with you? And don't take this the wrong way will you, Steve?

Steve Do my best.

Andrew Your confidence has taken a bit of a knock, hasn't it? These last few months.

Steve Has it?

Andrew You called it 'a little cut', didn't you?

Steve Well, it's just, the more I think about it –

Andrew Does it feel little when people aren't listening to a word y'saying?

Steve When they're what, sorry?

Andrew Does it feel little when passing strangers feel the need to look the other way?

Steve Passing strangers?

Andrew Because we're not just talking about physical scarring here are we, Steve?

Steve Aren't we?

Andrew How's the love life, Steve?

Steve Love life?

Andrew You're single, right?

Steve Possibly.

Andrew I mean I don't wanna point the figure, but Gillette have got an awful lot to answer for. D'you see what I'm saying, Steve?

Steve Not really.

Andrew Your confidence, Steve. Your confidence has taken a real blow.

Steve Has it?

Andrew We're talking psychological. Not literal scarring, Steve, but psychological. All because of one faulty razor. Personally, if it were me –

Steve Andrew, look, I appreciate your –

Andrew I bet you used to be a right ladies' man.

Steve I'm gay.

Andrew Exactly; man's man.

Steve Andrew, look, I really appreciate everything you've done –

Andrew Steve, listen to me, mate: I can't tell you how busy it is down here. There are literally not enough hours in the day. We are snowed under.

Steve As I say though, Andrew –

Andrew This isn't just about one faulty razor, Steve. What if it had been a child? What if it had been a little girl?

Steve Why would a little girl be shaving?

Andrew The point I'm trying to make, Steve –

Steve Andrew, Andrew, please –

Andrew Sorry, Steve, y' breaking up –

Steve Andrew –

Andrew Steve? Steve, are you there?

Steve I'm right here.

Andrew Oh no.

Andrew hangs up. Beat.

Kevin You remember when we was kids and we bunked off school that time? Year Ten. We was stood at the bus stop and you learned over to me and you said, (*whispers*) 'I've got a porno, let's sack this off.' I was fucking terrified. Started fucking sweating. And then the fucking *school* bus pitches up and you're all like, 'Mate, come on, 's fucking win-win.' So we do. We sack it off and we go to my mum's place. And we put it on. And I mean we're talking VHS, we're talking old-school porno. We're talking top-loader; proper old-school 'taches and tassels. And it's weird, innit? But we're both sat there with a couple teenage boners. 'S like *Kevin and Perry*. And then the door goes; the front fucking door. And I'm like a fucking lemur, like a fucking leopard, fucking bounding up and tryina rip that bloody video outta that machine. But we're busted, we are completely fucking –

Andrew Yeah, I remember.

Kevin You remember?

Andrew I remember.

Kevin My mum was fucking livid. Mean she was livid when you were there, but when you left, Jesus Christ, suddenly she was all fucking, 'You little effing this, you conniving effing that.'

Andrew Kevin, mate –

Kevin But no, look, listen, I'm serious cos I'm saying: wasn't it fucking thrilling. I always think of that y'know. No, don't look at me like that, I'm serious. That was one of the best fucking days of my life, no word of a lie. Now Andrew, I'm gonna say something and I want you to keep y' shit together while I do. I wasn't in an accident. Somebody was, just not me. I paid 'em, they had a prang, and then I came here.

Andrew 'S this a wind-up?

Kevin Deadly fucking serious.

Kevin slurps his coffee.

Andrew Bullshit.

Kevin Cross my heart and hope to die.

Andrew Careful what you wish for.

Kevin Blimey, thass a bit dark.

Kevin slurps his coffee.

I wanna start a business. Of sorts.

Andrew Kevin mate, I dunno how much you've had to drink –

Kevin I'm serious I'm serious –

Andrew 'S late, I gotta get a move on.

Kevin Listen, listen. Come on. There's this bloke called Bruno –

Andrew Bruno?

Kevin Yeah, Bruno.

Andrew Mate, he's having you on; nobody's called fucking Bruno anymore.

Kevin Bruno Alves, Bruno Tonioli. Bruno Mars.

Andrew I'm not interested.

Kevin Y' haven't even heard what I've gotta say?

Andrew Thanks for coming down, Kevin.

Kevin Don't be like that, don't be like that. Come on. Let's call him Dave, fuck it, we'll call him Dave. I've got this mate Dave and he knows everything there is to know about car crashes. He knows how to orchestrate 'em, he knows how to fake 'em and he knows how to make 'em up. He's got this whole network of people. But I'll be honest, I will be honest with you, Andrew, he's a grade-

A plonker. Thick as thieves, fucking literally, mate. But he's told me everything. He has told me absolutely bloody everything there is to know about it. So I went through him once to see how he did it and, credit where credit's due, he did an alright job. An' now I've got the knowledge –

Andrew How did he do it?

Kevin Mean the accident?

Andrew How'd he pull it off?

Kevin Two cars. Bruno – (*Corrects himself.*) *Dave* out in front, mate of his in the second.

Andrew Who?

Kevin Doesn't matter, some bloke. So they line up in front of this Tesco van and when they get to the roundabout, Dave breaks, fucking Stavros – Joe Bloggs – whatever he's called in the second car, my car, slams on the breaks, Tesco van goes inta the back of Joe Bloggs, and Bruno – (*Corrects himself.*) Dave drives off. Stavros has fucking nothing to do with it, we (*meaning he and Andrew*) put in the claim, Bruno's happy as Larry; no harm done.

Andrew Why d'you wanna do it?

Kevin Mate, look at me, I'm fucking skint. Business is fucking nose-diving, yet another fucking baby's on the way –

Andrew Get a loan.

Kevin If only. I've tried. You think I haven't tried?

Andrew I dread to think what you've tried.

Kevin 'S the climate. Everyone's battlin' it; fucking fiscal cliff, mate, and I'm hanging off the fucking edge. Listen I'm not talking old ladies and little kids. I'm talking people who can afford it. Fucking delivery vans, all that lot. Supermarkets. Fucking tax-dodgers. We find 'em, we follow 'em and we prang 'em. You know one pound in every fucking eight is spent in Tesco's? Saw that on fucking *QI*. And I don't even like *QI*, mate, but I saw that and I thought: thass not right.

Andrew Then stop going to Tesco's.

Kevin You think I can afford Tesco's? I'm a Morrisons man.

Andrew Can't stand Morrisons. Smells weird.

Kevin Mate: tell me about it.

  Beat.

Andrew Even if this were something I was interested in, which by the way it isn't, this is Barry's firm, 's not up to me.

Kevin Who said anything about telling Barry?

Andrew Barry's like a hawk.

Kevin Seems like a fucking teddy bear t' me.

Andrew I'm not lying to him.

Kevin Who said anything about lying?

Andrew (*beat*) You did.

Kevin Did I?

Andrew Just now.

Kevin What could you possibly be referring to?

Andrew ?

  Kevin playfully mimes zipping up his mouth. A telephone begins to ring. Answerphone kicks in.

Barry (*voice*) Thanks for calling Scorpion Claims. I'm sorry that neither myself nor my associate Andrew are here to take your call, but do please leave us a message and we'll get back to you as soon as we can.

Beep.

Steve (*voice*) Yeah, hello, Andrew it's Steve Beers here again. Uhhhm, Andrew I'm really sorry about this – You've been really – You really have – And I appreciate everything you've – But I think – For what it's worth, my instinct is that I'm going to pursue my claim elsewhere. I'm sorry, Andrew. Anyway, I'll . . .

Steve hangs up. Kevin finishes his coffee, downing it.

Kevin Time for one more?

Early to mid-autumn. Scorpion Claims. Night. Kevin, Guy and Anne. No light, except for any light that is spilling in from outside. Beat.

Anne Little old lady goes into HSBC and she says she wants to open a savings account. Person behind the counter says how much and the little old lady says three million quid. Person behind the till, the counter, understandably looks a little befuddled and she says in what form is the money? Little old lady slams a great big bag on the counter and says cash. Person behind the counter understandably thinks this all sounds a little fishy and goes to get the manager. Manager comes out, says hello to the little old lady and asks her where she got all this money. Little old lady says gambling; says I got it all from gambling. Gambling, says the bank manager, what sort of gambling? All sorts says the little old lady, anything and everything she says. I'll give you an example: I bet you that by midday tomorrow your balls will be square. Hundred grand, four-to-one odds. Bank manager says alright. Easy money, he thinks. Sure enough, little old lady pitches up the following day accompanied by some bloke. Bank manager greets her and says who's this? Little old lady says it's my lawyer; for a bet this big I'd rather have him present. Bank manager says I'm sorry to say my balls are indeed still round. Little old lady says not so fast; I'm sure you won't begrudge me double checking. Bank manager shrugs, undoes his belt and drops his trousers. Little old lady takes a hold of his balls and says you win, they're definitely not square. At that very moment, the little old lady's lawyer begins banging his head against the wall over and over. As the bank manager is pulling up his trousers, he says to the little old lady what's wrong with him, your lawyer, why's he banging his head against the wall? Well, says the little old lady –

Enter Andrew, with a torch.

Andrew Must be the power, definitely not the fuse.

Andrew picks up a telephone and places the receiver against his ear. It's dead.

Power. Bollocks.

Kevin Don't worry about it.

Andrew Is everyone warm enough?

Guy Fine. Thanks.　　　**Anne** Toasty.

Andrew Why don't we go around and introduce ourselves?

Kevin What?

Andrew Say who we are and where we're from.

Kevin Alright, Cilla, fucking hell. 'Number one: what's yer name and where d'ya come from . . .'

Anne It's polite.

Kevin No, yeah, mean – Just messing around.

Anne takes the torch from Andrew and holds it just below her face.

Anne My name's Anne. Black cab driver and lifelong Tory hater. Live in Batford. Husband's just been made redundant. Three daughters. (*Luton Town.*) Come on, you Hatters.

Anne passes the torch to Guy.

Guy Guy. Guy Haines. Run a professional mobile disco called Good Time Sounds. Uh, used to be a mechanic. Uh, yeah, thass it really.

Guy passes the torch to Kevin.

Kevin Kevin. Self-employed. Andrew and I were at school together. I am now married to a lovely lady named Jennifer who was in fact Andy's first lay.

Kevin is perhaps expecting some laughter, but there isn't any.

Bit of . . . bit of trivia for y' there.

Kevin hands the torch to Andrew.

Andrew My name's Andrew and I work here at Scorpion Claims.

Kevin 'S that it?

Andrew Does anyone have any questions before we get started?

Beat. Andrew takes a map (perhaps from a drawer) and unfolds it across one of the desks. Andrew shines the torch on a particular spot.

Can everyone see? This roundabout here joins the B653, the A505 and Gypsy Lane. It's one mile from junction ten of the M1, a matter of metres from Luton Airport Parkway, and as such it's a bit of a black-spot; we've certainly represented claimants in the past who have had accidents in this spot. Crucially, the roundabout itself is a stone's throw away from a retail park housing, amongst others, Toys R Us, B&Q and Next. The plan will be that you, Guy, in a hired car, will be driver number one, out in front, and that you, Anne, will be driver number two, behind Guy in your TX4. You'll be waiting in the car park of the retail park, preferably as near to the exit as possible. As and when either of you spot an LCV departing, you make sure you glide in ahead and proceed toward the aforementioned roundabout. Guy, as you approach the roundabout, you will begin to slow down. Anne, likewise. Guy, you will then break suddenly, forcing Anne to do likewise. The TX4 goes into the back of the hire car and, assuming all is well, the LCV will go into the back of the TX4. Now, this is the bit we haven't talked about. How would you feel about getting cut out of your TX, Anne?

Kevin Oh!

Anne Cut out?

Andrew By the fire service.

Kevin This is fucking gold.

Anne Why?

Kevin This. Is. Fucking.

Andrew More money.

Kevin Gold.

Andrew Be quiet.

Anne But what about m' car?

Andrew It'll all be covered.

Guy Why a hire car?

Andrew Would you rather wreck your own car?

Anne Well, hold on a minute: muggins here *is* wrecking her own car.

Guy Fair point.

Anne Yeah, I'll say –

Kevin Anne –

Anne Nobody mentioned cutting out when –

Kevin Anne, my darlin' –

Anne I'm speaking. I've sat through enough bloody *Casualty*, believe you me, to know what happens when you start cutting people outta cars.

Kevin Anne –

Anne I'm still speaking. I'm just letting you know now: I'm not up for losing a fucking limb. Pardon my French.

Kevin I'm not up for you losing a limb either, Anne; trust.

Guy Yeah, I have to say I think that would be a little unfair on Anne too.

Andrew No one's gonna lose anything, alright?

Anne (*beat*) Go on then, let's hear it.

Andrew What you'll have to do – No. What y'gonna have to do is t' ask *Guy* to call 999 on your behalf. You're frightened, there's a pain in your leg and you don't want to move. You're worried. Maybe you can even see some blood.

Anne Then what?

Andrew You wait. Happens all the time, promise ya.

Anne You mean w' fake accidents or real accidents?

Andrew Both.

Guy 'S there a passenger in the taxi?

Andrew No.   **Kevin** Yes.

Kevin What?

Andrew There's not a passenger in the taxi.

Kevin But I thought we'd talked about –

Andrew There's isn't a passenger.

Anne I don't want a passenger.

Kevin 'S that little bit more cash-dollar though, Anne.

Anne I'm not doing it with a passenger.

Kevin You'd know 'em.

Anne Oh.

Kevin We're not talking about an actual passenger.

Anne I'd know 'em or you'd know 'em?

Kevin Up to you. Choice is yours, my darling.

Andrew No passenger.

Andrew takes from a drawer a series of A4 handouts,
e.g. three or four sides stapled together. Andrew hands
them out.

There's more information on here. Much more detailed
outline and so on.

It's too dark to see the paper, so everyone takes out
their mobile telephones and uses the light from their
screens to read.

If you turn to the second page, you'll see an outline of
what needs to happen, what you need to do, on the day
after the collision. There's no need to go over it all now,
but the key thing to remember is that you mustn't go into
work and you must, I repeat must go and see your GP.

Guy What about the evening? I've got a bar mitzvah.

Andrew You'll have to cancel it. But only on the day.

Guy They're gonna be gutted.

Anne Couldn't we go the day after the day after?

Andrew It has to be the following day. A little lower down on page two, you'll see there's a list of the kinds of injuries we're going to need the two of you to be suffering from. Key areas: neck, shoulders and wrists. Keep it small; make sure you're really specific with the terms you use. Also –

Buzzer goes. Andrew wasn't expecting anyone.
Andrew checks his watch. Andrew takes the torch.

Kevin I'll go.

Andrew What?

Kevin I'll go.

Andrew You're not even s'posed to be here.

Andrew moves to go.

Kevin Okay, wait wait wait.

Andrew stops.

I thought we wanted a passenger so I found someone to be the passenger.

Andrew But we don't want a passenger.

Kevin I know, but I thought we did.

Andrew Who is it?

Kevin She's called Terri. She feeds my aunt's cousin's dog when they're away.

Andrew Fuck's sake.

Kevin Listen, I'm sorry, I swear to you I thought we'd said we wanted a passenger.

Buzzer goes again. Exit Andrew.

Guy He's a barrel of laughs that one.

Kevin Word on the street, Guy, is that he is currently in the middle of a fuck-off nasty divorce.

Guy Y' kidding?

Kevin 'Parently he hired a private detective.

Anne Don't be so ridiculous.

Guy How come?

Kevin Keep an eye on his missus.

Anne He was never married.

Kevin No, you're right, my darling he wasn't, but he coulda been. And what we've learnt, Anne, is you've got y'wits about ya; I like that.

Guy So why is he so bleedin' miserable?

Kevin Got the sack. Got caught fiddling something-or-other.

Guy Kids?

Kevin Jesus Christ, easy tiger. No, accounts; got caught fiddling the accounts. Some'in' like that anyway. Kids; fuck me.

Guy 'Member my first divorce; cost a bomb.

Anne How many more of these're there gonna be?

Kevin Terri's not even s'posed to be here –

Anne No – Accidents.

Kevin Loads. We wanna do loads, Anne. Many as you want, my darling. Big Society, innit. Bloke up north I heard about earned eighty grand. He was putting through one a week. Andy wants to start small, but I reckon once we get goin' we're not gonna be able to stop.

Anne And you reckon none of this'll ever make it to court?

Kevin Cost of challenging these claims is more than the cost of paying out. 'S not in their interests. And if we're smart, if we're fucking sharp, 'bout how we do it, 'bout what we're putting in for, 'bout who we're using, 'bout how we're diversifying: we'll be fine.

Anne I'm not gonna be able to keep crashing my cab.

Kevin And you won't need to. Once we're operating at a certain level, there won't even need to be an accident.

Guy You ever gonna be involved? Mean directly.

Kevin Absolutely. Try and stop me.

Enter Andrew and Terri. Terri is holding a blue plastic bag and wearing a bicycle helmet.

Oy-oy. How's it going?

Kevin greets Terri.

Terri Sorry I'm late. Stopped off at the offie.

Light resumes. For a moment, everyone finds it a little bright. Andrew turns off the torch.

Kevin What d'you get?

Terri Greene King.

Kevin What?

Anne IPA.

Kevin Less have a look.

Terri hands a can of Greene King IPA to Kevin.

Terri They brew it in Bury St Edmonds. 'S where the Magna Carta started.

Kevin What?

Terri Loada these barons met in the abbey in Bury St Edmonds and they drew up the first draft of the Magna Carta. Had a different title back then, but 's basically the same thing.

Kevin Nice.

Beat. Terri begins to introduce herself.

Terri (*to Guy*) Hiya, alright, how y'doing?

Guy Guy. Nice helmet.

Terri shakes Guy's hand and continues to do so.

Terri Yeah, thanks. Borrowed it off Ray from church. Used to be well inta his cycling till he got hit by that JCB an' that.

Guy nods; he has no idea how to respond. Guy breaks off the handshake.

Terri (*to Anne*) Hiya, alright.

Anne Hello, Terri, nice to meet you.

Terri and Anne begin to shake hands.

Terri Yeah no likewise.

Beat. Hand shaking continues.

Sorry, I didn't actually catch ya name?

Anne Anne.

Terri stops shaking Anne's hand and offers a hand to Andrew, which he doesn't accept.

Andrew Kevin, why don't you and Terri go and have a bit of a word?

Kevin What?

Andrew attempts a kind of covert 'look' to Kevin – i.e. 'We don't need a passenger; get rid of her.'

Kevin Mate, I dunno what y' on about?

Andrew Why don't you go and *update* Terri.

Kevin Still not with ya.

Andrew Fuck's sake – Terri, I'm sorry, there's been a bit of a mix-up. We don't need a passenger.

Kevin 'Kin hell. Yeah, look, sorry Terri –

Terri No, no, look, 's totally – 's totally –

Kevin Yeah, no, but listen, we are *definitely* gonna need –

Terri 'S fine, serious, 's totally fine. (*Beat.*) Nice t' meet you all.

Terri again shakes hands with Anne and Guy. It's a bit awkward, perhaps again it takes a touch too long. Terri holds out a hand for Andrew.

Anne Shake the girl's hand.

Andrew does so.

How big's ya bike, Terri?

Terri Whass that?

Anne If we can get it in the back o' me cab, give you a lift home if y'want?

Terri Get what in the back?

Anne (*perhaps gestures to Terri's helmet*) Y' bike.

Terri Haven't got a bike.

Anne ?

Terri Bang up a lift home though.

Anne Where y' heading?

Terri Marsh Farm.

Guy Blimey; no wonder y' wearing a fucking helmet.

Anne Go to church 'round there, do ya Terri?

Terri Holy Cross.

Anne Very nice.

Terri Coupla blindin' singers.

Anne Is that right. You sing?

Terri Yeah, little bit.

Anne What d'ya like t' sing?

Terri Hymns an' that.

Kevin I'll come down with ya.

Terri Don't worry about it.

Kevin Say hello to Sus for us, won't ya.

Terri Definitely.

Anne (*'Goodbye'*) Gentlemen.

Kevin offers to return the can of Greene King IPA to Terri.

Terri Keep it.

Anne (*as they're leaving*) My eldest sings . . .

Terri (*as they're leaving*) Oh yeah . . .

Exit Terri and Anne.

Kevin Why d'ya have to be such a cunt? D'you have any idea what she's been through this last year?

Guy (*beat*) Better make tracks. You'll text us a time for tomorrow?

Kevin We will.   .

Guy See you then.

*Exit Guy. Andrew opens the Greene King IPA and
drinks.*

Kevin Fuck.

Andrew What?

Kevin Forgot to ask 'bout the end o' that joke.

Andrew What?

*Late winter. Scorpion Claims. Day. Outside it is snowing.
Barry, seated, is scratching at scratch cards. After a
moment, enter Andrew.*

Andrew 'S he here?

Barry is focused on the scratch cards.

Barry.

Barry What's that?

Andrew 'S he here?

Barry Who?

Andrew Kevin.

Barry No.

Andrew Fuck're y' doing?

Barry Christmas millionaire.

Andrew Any luck?

Barry Gi' us a chance.

*Barry continues to scratch. Andrew moves to his desk
and peels off a Post-It note.*

Andrew What's this?

Barry Bollocks.

Andrew Barry.

Barry Yes mate.

Andrew holds up the Post-It note.

You had a call. Some bloke called Richard from financial protection. BUPA. Reckoned he was calling about y' dad. Told him he musta got his wires crossed.

Andrew When'd he call?

Buzzer goes.

Barry I'll go.

Exit Barry. Andrew moves to a telephone and, reading from the Post-It note, dials a number. Waits. Enter Barry and Kevin. Andrew hangs up.

Here he is, look.

Kevin Fuck me, 's colder in here than it is out there.

Andrew Barry, why don't you pop the kettle on?

Barry What d'ya fancy?

Kevin Barry: surprise me.

Barry You're on.

Exit Barry.

Kevin Wass going on?

Andrew Y' goin to court.

Kevin What?

Andrew Barry doesn't know – We're gonna – He doesn't know –

Kevin Hang on –

Andrew Listen to me. He doesn't know anything about anything. As far as he's concerned 's all legit.

Kevin Which claim are we talking?

Andrew Brilliant.

Kevin Don't be like that, come on, there's a fair few these days, let's face it.

Andrew Tesco.

Kevin Which one?

Andrew Your one, staged one. Delivery van. Near the Arndale.

Kevin One with Jen and Luce?

Andrew Yes.

Kevin I remember.

Andrew 'S being contested.

Kevin laughs, excited.

This isn't funny.

Kevin 'S a little bit funny – Of all the claims –

Andrew When Barry comes back in y' gotta pretend y' hearing all o' this for the first –

Kevin I'm on it. Relax brother.

Enter Barry with tea, hands it out.

Cheers, Bazza.

Kevin and Barry toast and drink.

Holy shit, that's good.

Andrew Thanks for coming to see us today, Kevin.

Kevin Andrew: always a pleasure.

Barry Kevin, mate, I'm just gonna be straight with ya, alright? Now there's no easy way to say this. Tesco and their insurers want to contest several elements of your claim. We've received instructions from the defence to attend a two-day trial at Luton County Court.

Kevin (*overdoing it*) You *what*? 'S this a wind-up?

Barry 'Fraid not.

Kevin Jesus H. Christ in a box. Thought you said there wouldn't be a trial?

Andrew That's as maybe, but –

Kevin You said we wouldn't have to go to court? When I came to you with this claim, Andrew, you said to me –

Andrew I know what I said.

Kevin 'S this a fucking joke to you?

Barry Alright.

Andrew Absolutely not.

Kevin (*overdoing it*) Fuck's sake, man; I'm in it up to my neck.

Barry Kevin, I need you to calm down and I need you to listen to me. What we're talking about here is a civil trial. Informal. Laid back. There's no need to panic.

Kevin Okay. Thanks, Barry. I'm sorry for raising my voice everyone.

He slurps his tea.

So how's it work?

Barry Good question.

Kevin Who's gonna be givin' evidence?

Andrew 'S gonna be you, Jen –

Kevin Jen? Whass Jen gotta do with it?

Barry Jen is one of the claimants.

Kevin But she was only a passenger?

Barry All claimants are required to attend.

Kevin She's gonna have to take time off work.

Barry Thass right.

Kevin Listen, I'm not being funny but we can't afford the time off.

Andrew Y' self-employed.

Kevin So?

Andrew Call in sick.

Kevin What about Jen?

Barry If y' claim is successful, any loss of earnings will be covered by the defence.

Kevin What if we don't wanna do it?

Andrew What?

Kevin Trial, what if we say no?

Barry Doesn't really work like that.

Kevin Well, they can't fucking make us, can they?

Barry Why wouldn't you wanna attend the trial?

Andrew He does.

Barry Kevin, why wouldn't you wanna continue pursuing this claim?

Kevin What if we get it wrong?

Andrew You won't.

Kevin But I'm saying if we do, on the day.

Barry 'S about evidence; not about getting it right or wrong.

Kevin I'm not a machine is all I'm saying, Barry.

Barry We understand. It is gonna be stressful, you're absolutely right. And I'm sorry about that. But what myself and Andrew are here to do is to prepare both yourself and Jennifer for every eventuality. No one's expecting the two of you to go through all of this alone.

Kevin What about Lucy?

Andrew No one likes to see children cross-examined. They'd be mad to request her.

Barry Cruel.

Andrew It'll just be yourself, and Jennifer.

Barry The defence.

Andrew And perhaps one or two witnesses.

Barry At most.

Andrew Alright?

Barry Now there is one other thing we need to speak to you about. If your claim is unsuccessful, then yourself and Jennifer will be liable for the entirety of the defence's fees. Cost of counsel, loss of earnings, any expert witnesses, et cetera, et cetera. With this in mind, we often recommend that our clients consider taking out something called After the Event Insurance.

Kevin (*not messing around*) What?

Andrew We can recommend a great firm that we use all the time and whom we trust.

Barry Temple.

Kevin How much is all this gonna fucking cost?

Andrew We'll look into to getting you an exact quote but, in all honesty, you're looking at somewhere in the region of between two and three thousand pounds.

Kevin You're having a fucking laugh.

Andrew If only.

Kevin Where d'you think we're gonna get two, three grand from? Shoe box under the fucking bed?

Andrew We appreciate it's an awful lot of money.

Kevin Don't patronise me, you fucking –

Barry Alright. Why don't we calm it down?

Kevin An' why don't you kiss my fucking arse? This is fucking daylight robbery.

Andrew Watch y' mouth.

Barry Let's just –

Andrew We're doing you a favour.

Kevin Most expensive fucking favour I've ever heard of.

Andrew You're a fucking Neanderthal, d'you know that?

Barry Alright –

Andrew D'you have any idea –

Barry Enough! 'S like being back at fucking school.

   Beat.

If your claim is successful, which, between you and me, I think it will be, all your costs will be covered. Now. We're aware that the cost of ATE Insurance might seem like a big ask, but, believe you me, it is absolutely worth it.

Kevin Why do we need insurance if y'reckon we're gonna win?

Barry 'S about protection.

Kevin We need this fucking money.

Andrew Don't we all.

Kevin Fuck's that s'posed to mean?

Beat.

So what happens now?

Andrew We'll be speaking to Jen –

Kevin You mean Jennifer.

Andrew What?

Kevin My wife, Jennifer. She's my wife, remember?

Andrew Fuck is wrong with you, are you low on sugar or something?

Beat.

Kevin Thanks for the tea, Barry.

Barry Why don't I walk you out?

Kevin Don't bother.

Exit Kevin, beat. Andrew moves to his desk, puts his jacket on, gathers his keys.

Andrew Goin'a Greggs, anything y' want?

Barry What was all that about?

Andrew All what about?

Barry Why's Humpty Dumpty getting his knickers in a twist?

Andrew (*beat*) Dunno.

Barry You alright? (*Beat.*) I'll have a muffin. Sticky Toffee.

Andrew Anything else?

Barry No, thanks.

Andrew moves to go.

Barry Actually, can y' get us some scratch cards?

Andrew More?

Barry Just a couple.

Andrew What y' after?

Barry Ace of Spades, Try Your Luck, Golden Bingo, Deal or No Deal.

Barry goes to hand Andrew a twenty-pound note.

Andrew They're on me.

Exit Andrew.

The following week. Scorpion Claims. Night. Still snowing perhaps. Andrew and Jennifer.

Jennifer I reckon you're about two feet taller, you know. Shot up. Like a rocket. Well, maybe not two feet, but. Must be something in the water. Mum always used to say that.

Andrew How is y' mum?

Jennifer Yeah, she's good thanks. Well. Keeping well. Trudging on. Soldiering through. Full steam ahead.

Andrew Give her my best.

Jennifer No, I will, I will. How's y' dad?

Andrew He's, uh, he's alright.

Jennifer You don't sound convinced?

Andrew He's been having a bit of trouble . . .

Jennifer (*beat*) Has he still got that great big beard of his?

Andrew No.

Jennifer He was like Big Foot. Wasn't he? Brian Blessed. Great big roaring laughter. Green giant. Hear him coming a mile off.

Andrew No, he's . . . not got the beard.

Beat.

Jennifer Look at your eyebrows. Right state.

Andrew Hold the phone.

Jennifer Used to be half the size. Used to look like shadows.

Jennifer gently straightens out/runs her finger along one of Andrew's eyebrows. Although this gesture begins innocently enough, it quickly becomes a touch too intimate. Beat.

Andrew Congratulations, by the way.

Jennifer ?

Andrew Hear you're expecting.

Jennifer Yes. Yep. Expecting. That's us. Bun in the oven. Summer baby. Don't know how I feel about it all, t' be honest with ya. Plus side, least it'll be nice and warm. Down side, he or she's gonna be a Cancerian.

Andrew How d'you mean?

Jennifer Cancer. Star sign. They're gonna be a crab. Little crab, staring up at ya.

Andrew Right.

Beat.

Jennifer Is it hot, are you hot?

Andrew 'S snowing.

Jennifer Sweating like a beast.

Andrew Take off y'jacket if y'want.

Andrew helps Jennifer remove her jacket. Again, this is perhaps curiously more intimate/awkward than either had expected.

Jennifer Nervous.

Andrew How d'ya mean?

Jennifer He's nice though, isn't he? Barry.

Andrew Yeah.

Jennifer With the tea. Barry with the tea. Missed you last coupla times I was here.

Andrew Yeah.

Jennifer Avoiding me, was ya?

Andrew What? Nah, just. Busy.

Jennifer Kev was saying he lives alone? Barry.

Andrew Was he.

Jennifer 'S he not got any family around?

Andrew Daughter lives up north.

Jennifer 'S she the one with the whadyacallit, degenerative thing?

Andrew Sort of.

Enter Barry with tea.

Barry Here we are.

Jennifer Ooh, lovely.

Barry Sorry it took s' long. Kettle's on the blink.

Jennifer Sure it'll be worth the wait. Good things come to those who . . .

Jennifer waits, and then laughs. Barry and Jennifer drink.

Blimey.

Barry What d'ya reckon?

Jennifer 'S like a little party.

Barry Good.

Andrew What can we do for ya, Jennifer?

Jennifer 'Jennifer'?

Andrew . . .

Jennifer Nobody calls me Jennifer. 'Part from Mum. You're so funny sometimes. Isn't he funny?

Barry He is.

Jennifer Funny little face.

Andrew Jen, is everything –

Jennifer I don't wanna go to court.

Andrew Okay.

Jennifer Please don't make me go to court.

Andrew You'll be fine. Won't she?

Barry Be over before y' know it.

Jennifer Can you please not make me go though?

Andrew What is it you're worried about?

Jennifer All of it. The whole thing.

Andrew Right.

Jennifer The oath.

Andrew How d'you mean?

Jennifer I was watching this thing on telly –

Andrew 'S not gonna be anything like –

Jennifer They make you swear, don't they?

Andrew They do, but –

Jennifer They give you a Bible, don't they?

Andrew You don't have to have a Bible if you don't wan' a Bible.

Jennifer Not been to church in years.

Barry Y' can take a non-religious oath, if y'd rather.

Andrew 'S all very modern.

Jennifer What do they use instead?

Andrew 'S just words.

Jennifer Mean I like the Bible, not saying I don't.

Andrew Then you should go for the Bible.

Barry Amen.

Andrew Listen, have a think.

Barry No rush.

Jennifer What happens if I lie?

Andrew Why would you lie?

Jennifer If I can't remember something –

Barry We talked about this, didn't we?

Jennifer No, I know.

Barry Jus' gotta say y' dunno.

Andrew Unfortunately, I am –

Barry Unable to recall –

Jennifer No, I know, I know. I know. But what happens if I've already lied?

Barry How d'you mean?

Andrew Y' just nervous.

Barry How d'you mean, love?

Andrew 'S just nerves.

Barry When would you've 'already lied'?

Jennifer The statement.

Barry What d'you mean? Are you saying you lied in the statement?

Jennifer Partly.

Barry Which part?

Andrew Alright –

Jennifer All of it.

Barry All of it?

Jennifer Yeah.

Barry It's, it's all a lie?

Jennifer Yeah.

Barry I'm – You . . . I'm just having a bit of trouble . . . It's all a lie, the whole statement?

Jennifer I'm so sorry, Barry, I'm so sorry. Andrew, I'm sorry.

Andrew You don't need to apologise.

Barry This is serious?

Jennifer Kevin paid someone to crash the car, or something. They do it for a living. These drivers. They follow old ladies around roundabouts all afternoon. Or they look for delivery vans. He didn't tell me about it. Until after it'd happened. He didn't tell me about it until after –

Andrew He didn't tell you about it?

Jennifer What?

Andrew You said he didn't tell you about it until *after* the accident?

Jennifer He told me what he'd done and he told me if I go along with it, there'll be a load more money. He said it would be easy. He said all I'd have to do is give a statement. He said these big faceless corporations usually just pay straight out. And then he told me about going to court and now I feel sick, I've been feeling sick –

Andrew It's okay.

Jennifer 'S not though, is it?

Andrew It is. 'S gonna be fine.

Jennifer Barry, I'm sorry.

Barry Don't be silly, love.

Andrew Can I just – I just wanna check something: you didn't know what was happening until after the accident?

Jennifer He said we had to go and see the GP.

Andrew Jen, I'm sorry.

Jennifer What've you got t' be sorry about?

Beat.

Barry Jesus Christ.

Beat.

Andrew Are you alright?

Jennifer Me?

57

Barry Who ya talking to?

Andrew Jen.

Jennifer Course I'm not alright – Feel like I been caught having a wank in the vet's.

Andrew Let's get you home.

Barry Lemme call you a taxi.

Jennifer 'S alright, y' don't have to –

Barry We insist.

Barry moves to a telephone, dials and orders a taxi during the following.

Andrew Will you do me a favour, Jen?

Jennifer ?

Andrew Can you not mention any of this to Kevin?

Jennifer Yeah, alright.

Andrew Don't tell him that we know what you know.

Jennifer zips her mouth.

Thanks.

Jennifer (*beat*) What're you thinking?

Andrew What?

Jennifer About, you, what're you thinking about?

Andrew I'm thinking about all sorts of things.

Jennifer Such as?

Andrew You.

Barry hangs up.

Barry On their way. D'you want a refill?

Jennifer Can I just have some water please, Barry?

Barry Course.

Barry takes Jennifer's cup and exits.

Jennifer What happens now?

Andrew How d'you mean?

Jennifer Now that you know.

Andrew Nothing. Nothing's gonna happen.

Enter Barry with a glass of water. Barry hands the water to Jennifer. Jennifer downs the whole glass.

Jennifer Thanks. Might wait outside?

Barry Sure? 'S freezing.

Jennifer Think I could do with the air. Feel a bit . . .

Barry I'll walk y' out.

Jennifer Don't be silly.

Jennifer puts on her jacket, zips it up. She exits. Barry moves to his desk, flicks through a stack of paper on his desk, lifts the receiver on his telephone and dials.

Andrew What y'doing?

Barry Wass it look like? Giving that motherfucker a –

Andrew Don't.

Barry Can't believe –

Andrew Hang up the phone.

Andrew moves to the telephone and ends the call.

Barry What y'doing?

Andrew Why y'calling him?

Barry Tell him he can shove his claim up his fucking –

Andrew Why?

Barry You stoned or some'ing? 'S bullshit, 's a bullshit claim.

Andrew So?

Barry So we're not going near it.

Andrew Why not?

Barry Because 's fraud.

Andrew Never bothered you before.

Barry Fuck's that s'posed t' mean?

Andrew I'm just saying, Barry.

Barry Now hang on a minute; I have never knowingly –

Andrew Ah, bullshit. Arthur Garfield ring any bells? Antonio DeSilva, Michael Pakulski, thingy Patel, Will Baker –

Barry Fuck you on about?

Barry There may have been times when I had a creeping suspicion that

Andrew 'Creeping suspicion'? one or two minor elements of a particular claim –

Andrew 'One or two minor elements' – Jesus Christ, Barry, we took on a woman who reckoned her boobs exploded.

Barry *One* of her boobs. That was a legitimate –

Andrew Listen I have thought about this and I have thought about this and you wanna know how I feel about it?

Barry What d'ya mean, you've thought about it?

Andrew Who gives a fuck if some behemoth of an insurance company, who look after one of the biggest supermarket chains in the –

Barry What d'ya mean, you've –

Andrew Who, by the way, probably don't even pay their –

Barry What d'ya mean, you've thought about it, how have y'thought about it? Motherfucker only juss told us.

Andrew I'm saying in the abstract.

Barry No y'not.

Andrew Oh come off it, Barry, give me some fucking credit. You think if I had anything to do with that weaselly motherfucker and his drop-in-the-ocean claim I wouldn't't've spruced it up a bit? I'm saying generally speaking. There is a culture. That exists. And whether you or I like it or not –

Barry Who said anything about –

Barry This is my firm.

Andrew Sorry t' have t' be the one to break it to ya, Barry, only reason 's your firm is cos the bloke who used to run it died.

Barry 'S also the only reason you're not out of a fucking job, so show a bit o' respect. I'm not fucking around, Andrew. That shit goes on, I'm not sayin' it doesn't. But I'll be fucked if it goes on here.

Andrew You're seriously tryin'a –

Barry I haven't finished. Now did you or did you not know this claim was bullshit?

Andrew Come off it, Barry –

Barry Look at me when I'm talking to ya. You knew he was lying, yes or no? (*Beat.*) Don't devalue us, Andrew.

Andrew No. I didn't know.

Beat.

Barry I'm goin'a Greggs.

Exit Barry. Andrew, alone. Telephone begins to ring. Andrew lets it ring for a moment, unsure whether he wants to answer. He answers using speakerphone.

Andrew Scorpion Claims, Andrew speaking.

Graham (*voice*) Andrew? 'S Dad.

Andrew picks up the receiver.

Andrew (*into phone*) Hello. Dad. Yeah, I'm alright. You?

Andrew listens.

(*Into phone.*) Yeah, no, I spoke to one of the nurses about it and she said she's gonna –

Andrew listens.

(*Into phone.*) I'll bring you a coupla magazines tonight. Yeah, no.

Andrew listens.

(*Into phone.*) Alright, I'll see you later. Alright. Yeah, take care.

Andrew hangs up.

Two

*Summer. Luton County Court, approaching ten thirty a.m.
Day one of the trial. The weather outside and in the
courtroom itself are extremely hot. Andrew, Barry,
Georgina, Isabella and Attendant. Everyone is waiting,
checking their watches, anxious, sweaty, twiddling their
thumbs, etc. Andrew and Barry drink coffee from
Greggs; Georgina and Isabella drink coffee from
Starbucks. Georgina takes out her mobile telephone
(preferably a very modern model) and dials.*

Georgina (*into phone*) Liza, it's Georgina. I'm sorry we
didn't get a chance to speak last night. But, look, Tom
and I would really love to see you all at the weekend. I'm
in court all day, but I'll be at home tonight. Alright, lots
of love.

> *Georgina hangs up. Andrew and Georgina smile
> politely at one another.*

Andrew 'S hot.

Georgina Beg your pardon?

Andrew It's hot. In here.

Georgina Yes. I think there's a problem with the air
conditioning.

Andrew Is that right?

Georgina I think so.

Andrew So I noticed that you, you changed counsel?

Georgina That's right.

Andrew We were expecting –

Georgina Matthew, that's right.

Andrew Younger.

Georgina Yes, that's right, this would have been his first trial. He was really upset.

Barry Not the only one.

Andrew Some sort of problem, was there?

Georgina Glandular fever.

Barry Nasty.

Georgina Indeed.

Andrew Still it's really great to. Meet you.

Georgina Likewise.

Andrew Heard a lot about you.

Georgina Have you?

Barry Ball-breaker.

Georgina Excuse me?

Andrew We've heard you don't pull any punches.

Georgina's mobile telephone begins to ring:

Georgina Would you excuse me. (*Into phone.*) Liza, hello, how are you? Oh, please, don't be silly. No, that sounds lovely. Tom's really excited. Sounds wonderful. No, please, let me bring something. You're sure? I'll cobble something together. Please, it's the least I could do. Alright, speak soon. Yeah, take care. Lots of love.

Andrew 'Ball-breaker'?

Barry What?

Andrew D'you wanna try giving 'em another ring? Mean this is fucking crazy.

Barry begins to dial.

Georgina hangs up.

64

Barry (*into phone*) Hello, Kevin, it's Barry. Barry from Scorpion Claims. (*Beat. To Andrew.*) They're outside.

Andrew Go and get 'em.

Barry (*into phone*) Yeah, I'm coming to get you. Yeah, just go through the metal detector and then – Yeah, that's it.

Exit Barry.

Andrew Tom y' husband?

Georgina I'm sorry?

Andrew Tom, is he your . . . he your partner?

Georgina Tom is my son's name.

Andrew (*gesturing towards Georgina's mobile, genuinely surprised*) You on the internet?

Georgina They have wireless.

Andrew In here? Y' joking?

Georgina You can get the password from reception.

Andrew Worth knowing.

Georgina Yes.

Andrew Not least cos the fucking dongle's on the blink.

Georgina There's a phrase you don't hear very often.

Andrew ?

Enter Barry, Kevin and Jennifer. Jennifer's baby is due any day now.

Barry Here they are.

Kevin Sorry we're late. Right fucking nightmare.

Andrew What happened?

Kevin Traffic was hellish.

Andrew No shit.

Georgina Are we ready?

Barry All set.

During the following, Georgina informs the Attendant that all are ready to begin. Exit Attendant.

Andrew (*to Kevin*) Where's y' suit?

Kevin You what?

Andrew Y' suit. We told you to wear a suit.

Kevin 'S too hot.

Andrew What d'ya mean?

Kevin Fucking ninety degrees.

Andrew I didn't ask you for a fucking weather report. Asked y' t'come appropriately dressed.

Barry Alright.

Barry reaches into a pocket, takes out a tie and hands it to Kevin.

Put this on.

Enter Attendant.

Attendant All rise.

Barry helps Kevin put on the tie as Judge Jessup enters. Jessup carries with him a portable fan that requires plugging in. Once Jessup is seated (he nods before doing so), everyone else takes their seats.

Jessup So, here we are. Good morning, everyone. First things first: as I'm sure you will have detected, the air conditioning seems to have once again let us down. I hope you won't mind, therefore, that I am accompanied today by a very good friend of mine. We spent the best part of last week together and I can assure you that he is nowhere near as disruptive as you might think.

Jessup plugs in the fan and switches it on; a smile creeps across his face.

Now, I always like to begin by reminding those of you that have been kind enough to grace us with your presence, that this is not a criminal trial. We are in a civil court. You mustn't, therefore, worry or make yourselves anxious unnecessarily. I know from personal experience that giving evidence can be a very nerve-wracking moment in one's life. However, it is important to remember that your statements given prior to this trial are finite. We are not here today to test one another's memory. Errors and omissions are not our concern. So, please, relax and let's be as speedy as we can.

Kevin enters the witness box. Attendant holds out a laminated oath from which Kevin reads the following.

Kevin (*leans in and speaks very closely to the microphone*) I swear by Almighty God that the evidence I give shall be the truth, the whole truth, and nothing but the truth.

Andrew Would you state your name please?

Kevin, again, leans in and speaks very closely to the microphone:

Kevin Kevin Needleman.

Andrew Your date –

Jessup Sorry to interrupt, Mr Eagleman.

Andrew Not at all, Your Honour. The floor is yours.

Jessup Now Mr Needleman, please don't feel that you have to lean in like that towards the microphone. I can assure you that the recording equipment in this courtroom is more than capable of picking you up from a safe distance, as it were.

Kevin Right you are.

Jessup Mr Eagleman.

Andrew Thank you, Your Honour. What is your date of birth?

*Kevin automatically leans into the microphone but
tries to sit back as soon as he catches himself doing this.*

Kevin February the – Sorry. February the second, nineteen eighty.

Andrew And is everything in your statement true to the best of your knowledge?

Kevin Yeah.

Andrew No further questions.

Georgina Mr Needleman, had you been involved in a road traffic accident prior to the collision which took place on July twelfth, two thousand and twelve?

Kevin No.

Georgina You're certain of that fact, Mr Needleman?

Kevin Hundred and ten per cent.

Georgina I have here in front of me, Mr Needleman, an email from a Mr James Macdonald of Arnold Mitchell which I'm afraid to say says otherwise. According to Mr Macdonald, in two thousand and eleven you submitted a personal injury claim –

Kevin Right, no, yeah – Well I mean there's that one. Yeah I mean if we're talking two thousand eleven, then you're bang on.

Georgina It must have slipped your mind.

Andrew Your Honour, Miss Burns seems to be rather unnecessarily, not to mention cruelly, passing judgement on Mr Needleman, with –

Jessup Is she?

Andrew Your Honour, my client is allowed to forget.

Jessup And Miss Burns is allowed to comment on said forgetfulness, is she not, Mr Eagleman? Miss Burns.

Georgina Thank you, Your Honour. Mr Needleman, what were yourself, your wife and your daughter doing when the accident of July twelfth took place?

Kevin We were driving.

Georgina Evidently. What was the purpose of your journey, Mr Needleman?

Kevin Shopping.

Georgina Can you be a little more specific?

Kevin We was out tryin'a find a present for Lucy.

Georgina And did you?

Kevin Come again?

Georgina Did you find a present, for your daughter?

Kevin Dunno.

Georgina You don't know?

Kevin Mean what does it say in the statement?

Georgina Well, interestingly enough, Mr Needleman, it doesn't.

Kevin Guess we didn't find anything then.

Georgina Evidently.

Kevin Mighta been the cinema.

Georgina I beg your pardon, Mr Needleman?

Kevin I was sayin': It Might Have Been The *Cinema*.

Georgina As opposed to shopping?

Kevin Cineworld, thass what I'm saying.

Georgina What were you hoping to see?

Kevin I dunno, it was fucking a year ago, you tell me.

Jessup Mr Needleman, I think we can do without that kind of language today if you don't mind.

Kevin Sorry, 's just – Mean, you just said we're not on trial.

Jessup That's correct.

Kevin So why's she fucking gunning for me?

Andrew Your Honour, I wonder if it's worth mentioning –

Jessup Mr Eagleman –

Andrew Your Honour, Mrs Needleman is days away from giving birth, this is an extremely stressful time for my clients.	**Georgina** Your Honour, I don't really see what relevance this has –

Jessup Alright, alright. Why don't we all just take a moment and catch our breaths. Miss Burns, perhaps you would be so kind as to ever-so-slightly soften your tone. Mr Needleman, once again, if you could refrain from swearing in my courtroom it would be greatly appreciated. And Mr Eagleman, I thank you for your concern for your clients, but why don't we see if we can't all *stick to the script*, as it were.

Andrew (*meaning 'of course'*) Your Honour.

Jessup Miss Burns.

Georgina Thank you, Your Honour. In your statement, Mr Needleman, you claim that, immediately following the collision, you vacated your car, is that correct?

Kevin Yeah, thass right.

Georgina What were you doing?

Kevin Speaking to the driver of the van.

Georgina And how were you feeling at this point?

Kevin You know, angry. Upset. Bit tense.

Georgina And your wife and daughter were still seated inside the car, is that right?

Kevin Yeah.

Georgina At what point did you check on them?

Kevin When I got back in the car.

Georgina Your first instinct, then, was to vacate the car?

Kevin Not sure I'm followin'?

Georgina At what point did you check on the health of your wife and daughter?

Kevin When I got back into the car.

Georgina And how long were you absent from the car?

Kevin Five, maybe ten minutes?

Georgina Five, maybe ten minutes?

Kevin Some'in' like that, yeah.

Georgina And when you returned to the car, how were your wife and daughter?

Kevin They were pretty shaken up.

Georgina Can you be a little more specific?

Kevin Lucy was crying and Jen, she was looking after her.

Georgina Your wife was looking after your daughter?

Kevin Yeah.

Georgina In what way?

Kevin She was, you know, cuddling her, stroking her.

Andrew reacts to this.

Georgina Your wife was 'cuddling' and 'stroking' your daughter?

Kevin Yes, ma'am.

Georgina In your wife's statement, Mr Needleman, she claims that your daughter was seated in the back seat of your car?

Kevin Yeah, she was.

Georgina Where was your wife seated, Mr Needleman?

Kevin In the front.

Georgina Your wife states that she remained in the front seat of the car following the collision.

Kevin So?

Georgina How did your wife manage to, in your words, Mr Needleman, cuddle and stroke your daughter from the front seat of the car, whilst your daughter was seated in the back?

Kevin How d'you mean?

Georgina I'm just wondering about the physics of cuddling and stroking someone who is seated some one to two feet behind you?

Kevin I didn't mean literally.

Georgina Oh, you didn't mean literally?

Kevin She was sort of saying stuff, you know.

Georgina 'She was sort of saying stuff'?

Kevin Yeah, I'm saying, she wasn't – I mean she wasn't

literally hugging her. She wasn't *literally* holding her.

Georgina She wasn't?

Kevin No.

Georgina Oh, I see. I didn't realise we were responding to one another metaphorically, Mr Needleman. My apologies.

Georgina's wit/sarcasm momentarily stumps Kevin.

How was your wife expressing her concern?

Kevin Speaking and that.

Georgina And how did you express your concern?

Kevin Same, yeah, speaking and that.

Georgina And how did your wife and your daughter respond to your speaking and that?

Kevin Well, Jen was sort of putting on a bit of a brave face and that. But, Lucy, she was . . . you know . . . She started complaining about a pain in her neck.

Georgina Your daughter was complaining of a pain in her neck?

Kevin Yeah.

Georgina And this is all some five, ten minutes after the collision itself?

Kevin Yeah. Maybe fifteen, maybe twenty.

Georgina 'Maybe fifteen, maybe twenty'?

Kevin Yeah, I'm saying, fuck me, it could've been. Mean it could've been anything.

Jessup Mr Needleman –

Kevin No, but I'm saying, when you're in that sort of situation, when y' shaken up and y' worried, the last thing y' worryin' about is the fucking time, d'you know what I mean?

Jessup We certainly do, Mr Needleman. But, once again, I would urge you to refrain from using language of a, shall we say, coarse nature toward Miss Burns.

Georgina (*meaning 'thank you'*) Your Honour. How did you respond to your daughter's complaint about her neck?

Kevin I said it hurts, does it? And she said yeah. And I said whereabouts? And she said here. (*Gestures to the back of his neck, between his shoulder blades.*) And then, when we got in, we gave her some squash and we put her to bed.

Georgina How old is your daughter, Mr Needleman?

Kevin She's four.

Georgina On July thirteenth, the day after the collision, your daughter continued to complain of both head and neck pain, is that correct?

Kevin Yeah.

Georgina You took your daughter to see your local GP on July nineteenth, is that correct?

Kevin It is. Big time.

Georgina A whole week later?

Kevin What?

Georgina I'm trying to ascertain, Mr Needleman –

Kevin We had a holiday booked.

Georgina A holiday?

Kevin Family visit.

Georgina A pre-planned family visit or an impromptu family visit?

Kevin Pre-planned.

Georgina How far were you travelling?

Kevin Weymouth; visit m'dad's side of the family.

Georgina Yourself, Mrs Needleman and your daughter all travelled to Weymouth in the days following your collision?

Kevin Exactly. We didn't wanna delay it cos we don't get down there enough as it is. An' I know what y' gonna say, y' gonna say, 'But Mr Needleman I thought y'daughter was injured?' Yeah, well, y'know what? Kids complain about shit all the time.

Andrew reacts to this.

Fact. They like a fucking moan. Now fine, maybe I shoulda taken it more seriously, but I'm a family man and I believe we have a *responsibility* to keep up certain family ties, particularly ones that are on the verge of fuckin' severin'. So fine, I mighta fucked up in terms o' Luce and keepin' an eye on her, but that's all it is.

Georgina Are you suggesting, Mr Needleman, that your daughter's injuries were perhaps not as serious as you initially thought?

Andrew Your Honour –

Kevin No, I'm saying: we didn't *think* they were that serious because kids complain about stuff all the time. I'm saying we didn't think they were that serious because we just get on with things. And it was only *after*, when we got *back*, that I realised Luce had been pretty seriously affected.

Georgina And when was that?

Kevin What?

Georgina When exactly did you realise the severity of your daughter's injuries?

Kevin When we went to the fu— When we took her to the GP.

Georgina On July nineteenth?

Kevin *Yes.*

Georgina And how did you travel to Weymouth, Mr Needleman? In light of the damage to your car following your collision.

    Beat.

Georgina Mr Needleman?

Kevin I'm listenin'.

Georgina As am I. Indeed, as are we all. Can I suggest to you, Mr Neddleman, that your daughter wasn't actually present at the time of the collision?

Kevin What?

    Kevin looks towards Andrew, stunned, bemused, unsure how to respond.

Andrew *Say something.*

Jessup Mr Eagleman –

Kevin Course she was. Mean course she fucking was.

Jessup Mr Needleman, please.

Kevin Look if you wanna fucking *harangue* me for not looking after Luce, then, fine, y'know, fine. Fair enough. Maybe I was a bit, mean maybe I was a bit, fucking, dismissive. But I don't really see what that has to do with the fact that, actually, y' know, fucking, actually, that the main reason for us not sorta fucking

Jessup Mr Needleman –

Jessup Mr *Needleman* –

Jessup Mr Eagleman, would you kindly ask

doing anything about it, is cos we didn't wanna make a fucking fuss! And fucking grilling me and fucking grilling me – I mean whass y' fucking problem? I mean how much fucking – No I mean I'm being serious, how much fucking money d'you lot make? *She shunted into the back of us.* End of story.

your client to refrain from –

Andrew Kevin –

Andrew *Kevin.*

Andrew *Stop talking*!

Beat.

Georgina No further questions.

Later that same day. Jennifer is in the witness box, about to take an oath.

Jennifer Can I, actually, sorry, I, I requested the non-religious one. (*To Jessup.*) If that's okay?

Jessup Of course.

    Attendant holds out a laminated oath from which Jennifer reads the following:

Jennifer I . . . Insert name do – I, Jennifer Needleman, do solemnly, sincerely and truly declare and affirm that the evidence I give shall be the truth, the whole truth and nothing but the truth.

Andrew Would you state your name please?

    Jennifer vomits. She tries to catch the vomit in her hands. It's not a great deal of vomit, but it nonetheless spurts from her mouth and trickles through her fingers. Various people – Attendant, Barry, Andrew et al. – immediately move towards the witness box. Andrew manages to get to the witness box before Kevin.

77

Jennifer Oh God, I'm sorry, I'm so sorry.

Jessup You mustn't apologise, Mrs Needleman. Sometimes, all one can do is let Mother Nature have her way. Is there anything that we can get you?

Jennifer I think it might have been the water. It's really warm. If you had some ice, or if you had some from a bottle, that might be better.

Jessup Of course.

Exit Attendant.
    Andrew and Jennifer, close:

Andrew You alright?

Jennifer (*nods*) Yeah.

Andrew Are you sure?

Jennifer Yeah, yeah I'm fine – We had fish – Last night – I knew we shouldn't have – We got a takeaway from that place run by that old Chinese woman? They do fish and they do chips but then they do spring rolls and chow mein.

Andrew Okay.

Jennifer I've always thought it was weird.

Andrew Yeah, it sounds it.

Enter Attendant with some kitchen paper and a chilled bottle of water. Andrew helps Jennifer clean herself up, etc.

Jennifer Andrew, I'm fucking petrified.

Andrew Don't be. Listen to me, listen to me: y'gonna be fine. Alright? Y'gonna be fine.

Without thinking, as it were, Andrew pecks Jennifer on the cheek. Andrew returns to his seat. Kevin glares.

Jessup How would you feel about giving that another go, Mrs Needleman?

Jennifer No, definitely. Definitely.

Jessup Mr Eagleman.

Andrew (*meaning 'thank you'*) Your Honour. Would you state your full name ,please?

Jennifer Jennifer Louise Cynthia Needleman.

Andrew And would you state your date of birth please?

Jennifer The twenty second of January nineteen eighty.

Andrew And, to the best of your knowledge, is everything in your statement true?

Jennifer Yes.

Andrew No further questions.

Georgina Mrs Needleman, earlier on, your husband was having trouble remembering what had prompted your trip to the Arndale Shopping Centre on –

Jennifer He'd forget his head if it wasn't screwed on.

Georgina I see.

Jennifer *Men.*

Georgina Indeed.

Jennifer We have this enormous calendar in our kitchen –

Georgina (*pressing on*) Mrs Needleman, I was wondering if you might be able to shed a little more light on what exactly prompted the excursion in question?

Jennifer It was a DVD.

Georgina A DVD?

Jennifer *Up.*

Georgina I beg your pardon?

Jennifer It's a film. *Up.* It's a film for children.

Georgina I see, yes. I am indeed familiar with the film *Up.*

Jennifer We saw it when it was out in 3D. We both really loved it. Kevin didn't come.

Georgina You don't mention any of this in your statement, Mrs Needleman?

Jennifer Nobody really asked.

Georgina 'Nobody really asked'?

Jennifer Not really, no.

Georgina In your statement, Mrs Needleman, you claim that, following the collision, you remained in your seat?

Jennifer That's correct.

Georgina Your daughter was seated in the back seat –

Jennifer Yes.

Georgina And you were seated in the front passenger seat?

Jennifer That's correct.

Georgina Your husband vacated the car almost immediately after the collision?

Jennifer He did.

Georgina In your statement, Mrs Needleman, you state that your husband refers to the defendant as an 'effing dozy c-word'?

Jennifer That's correct.

Georgina You hear this?

Jennifer That's correct.

Georgina You are seated inside your vehicle and you are able to hear your –

Jennifer Yeah, I hear it.

Georgina Were any of the windows open at this point?

Jennifer No.

Georgina He must have been speaking quite loudly?

Jennifer His door was open.

Georgina His door was open?

Jennifer That's correct.

Georgina I just *asked* you, Mrs Needleman –

Jennifer You said windows. You asked if any of the windows were open.

Georgina I see.

Jennifer You didn't ask about doors.

  Andrew smiles.

Georgina After vacating your car, your husband left his door ajar?

Jennifer That's correct.

Georgina But you remained in your seat?

Jennifer Yes.

Georgina In your statement you state that your daughter was 'crying'?

Jennifer That's correct.

Georgina And yet you didn't feel compelled to leave your seat at any point?

Jennifer I don't understand?

Georgina I'm just trying to understand why, given that both yourself and your husband lay claim to the fact that your daughter, four years of age at the time –

Jennifer I think I was in shock.

Georgina You *think* that you were in *shock*?

Jennifer . . .

Georgina Mrs Needleman?

Jennifer Yes.

Georgina The word 'shock' isn't mentioned in your –

Jennifer I put my hand behind me, behind my seat.

Georgina You put your hand behind you?

Jennifer Yes.

Georgina Meaning what exactly?

Jennifer To reach for Lucy, to reach for her. To make sure she was okay.

Georgina To make sure that your daughter was uninjured –

Jennifer Okay, to make sure that she was –

Georgina I'm sorry, Mrs Needleman, I'm not quite sure I'm clear on –

Jennifer I reached for her hand. I reached behind, behind my seat, to hers, and I grabbed her by the hand. Held it, clutched it.

Georgina You don't mention any of this in your statement?

Jennifer Yeah.

Georgina I'm sorry?

Jennifer I said I know. I don't.

Georgina Were you saying anything to one another?

Jennifer Yeah.

Georgina What were you saying?

Jennifer I was . . . Things like . . . 'Are you okay?' 'Does anything hurt?' That sort of thing.

Georgina And how did your daughter respond?

Jennifer I don't know.

Georgina You don't know?

Jennifer I can't really remember.

Georgina Why ever not, Mrs Needleman?

Andrew Your Honour, please, Counsel's question is –

Jessup Miss Burns, I'm afraid Mr Eagleman might have a point, as it were. We are not here to test one another's ability to recall information.

Georgina I apologise, Your Honour. Why didn't you, say, physically *move* to comfort your daughter directly?

Andrew Your Honour, please, again, Counsel is pushing the claimant –

Jessup Well, yes, indeed I see where you are coming from, Mr Eagleman, but, even so –

Andrew Your Honour, all of this is covered in my client's statement –

Jessup Indeed it is –

Andrew My client has already stated that she was both in shock at the time and is now unable to remember.

Jessup Nonetheless, Mr Eagleman, *none the less*. Miss Burns.

Georgina Thank you, Your Honour. When did your daughter first mention to you that she was suffering from any kind of pain?

Jennifer The morning after the crash.

Georgina The morning *after* the collision?

Andrew reacts to this.

Jennifer Yeah.

Georgina And yet, despite this, despite repeated complaints from your daughter Lucy, you still decided to get in the car and drive to Weymouth?

Jennifer I didn't. And they didn't take the car. Lucy likes the train. Plan was always to take the train.

Georgina You're saying you did not travel to Weymouth?

Jennifer No, I couldn't get the time off.

Georgina You couldn't get the time off for a pre-planned, family holiday?

Jennifer That's correct.

Georgina sips some water. She flips through her case 'bundle'.

Georgina When did the idea of putting in a claim arise?

Jennifer I can't recall.

Georgina How did yourself and your husband know that you might be entitled to compensation?

Jennifer I don't understand?

Georgina Where did the idea of putting in a claim stem from?

Jennifer It didn't really stem from anywhere. You just know.

Georgina How does one 'just know', Mrs Needleman?

Jennifer 'S everywhere.

Georgina What is?

Jennifer Those adverts.

Georgina Adverts?

Jennifer Yeah.

Georgina Personal injury advertisements?

Jennifer Yeah.

Georgina And was it following one of these 'adverts' that it occurred to yourself and Mr Needleman that you might be *on to a winner*?

Andrew Jen, you don't have to answer that. Your Honour –

Jessup Perhaps a touch too gauche, Miss Burns.

Georgina Apologies, Your Honour. No further questions.

Beat.

Jennifer Is that it?

Jessup That is indeed *it*. Thank you, Mrs Needleman.

Jennifer looks around the courtroom briefly.

I hate those adverts. By the way. I think they're really warped.

Jennifer leaves the witness box.

The following day, approaching ten a.m. Kevin, Andrew and Barry, coffee from Greggs. Attendant perhaps also present. Enter Georgina and Isabella, frappuccinos from Starbucks – lots of cream, straws, whole deal. The temperature is still roasting.

Andrew Morning.

Georgina Good morning.

Barry Sleep alright?

Georgina Very well thank you. Yourself?

Barry Like a log.

Andrew What y'drinking?

Georgina This is a caramel frappuccino.

Andrew Oh yeah. Any good?

Georgina Delicious.

Georgina sucks her frappuccino through a straw. Andrew and Barry watch.

Barry Y'ever been t' Greggs?

Georgina I have to confess, I don't think that I have.

Barry Wanna think about poppin' y'head in; do a crackin' pan o' choc'late.

Georgina perhaps slurps the remainder of her frappuccino, finishing it.

Georgina I'm afraid I don't buy the holiday story.

Andrew Come again?

Georgina The holiday story; I don't buy it.

Barry I'm sorry to hear that.

Attendant All rise.

As with day one, Jessup enters, nods, everyone takes their seats and he plugs in his fan.

Jessup Good morning, everyone. I trust everyone had a good night's sleep, as it were. Miss Burns.

Georgina (*meaning 'thank you'*) Your Honour.

Isabella enters the witness box. Attendant holds out a laminated oath from which Isabella reads the following:

Isabella I swear by Almighty God that the evidence I give shall be the truth, the whole truth, and nothing but the truth.

Georgina What is your full name?

Isabella Isabella Sue-Ellen Reynolds.

Georgina What is your date of birth?

Isabella The second of the seventh nineteen ninety-one.

Georgina And to the best of your knowledge, is everything in your statement true?

Isabella Yeah, it is, yeah.

Georgina No further questions.

Andrew Miss Reynolds, how long have you worked as an online delivery driver?

Isabella Not that long. Not that long at all really.

Andrew Are you in full-time employment?

Isabella The delivery job is part-time.

Andrew You've another job as well, is that right?

Isabella Yeah, I work at Verdi's.

Andrew Verdi's?

Isabella Yeah, 's an Italian restaurant.

Andrew What are the terms of your employment with Verdi's?

Isabella I do . . . Well. it sorta depends.

Andrew On what does it depend?

Isabella Well, I mean in theory, right, I'm only down to do week nights and every other weekend.

Andrew Why only in theory?

Isabella Well, the other girl that works there, right, she's Gennaro's daughter.

Andrew Gennaro?

Isabella Yeah, he's the owner.

Andrew He's the owner.

Isabella Yeah, and the thing is, right, his daughter, Cheryl (I know, grim) she's got this boyfriend –

Andrew Cheryl has a boyfriend?

Isabella Duncan.

Jessup Mr Eagleman, are you planning on developing this particular line of questioning at any point in the not too distant future?

Andrew (*meaning 'Come again?'*) Your Honour?

Jessup Fascinating as Miss Reynolds' personal life is, I'm not quite sure how vital it is to this particular enquiry.

Andrew . . .

Jessup Do feel free to *move things along*.

Andrew Your delivery job is a day job, would that be fair to say?

Isabella Yeah, definitely.

Andrew And your job with Verdi's is predominantly evenings?

Isabella Five thirty till eleven thirty.

Andrew What time would you normally start your day job?

Isabella Depends.

Andrew How so?

Isabella Thursdays and Fridays I start at, like, nine and Mondays I start at ten.

Andrew You must be quite tired then?

Isabella What's that?

Andrew Finishing one job at eleven thirty and beginning another at nine, must be quite a tiring routine?

Isabella Yeah, I mean sometimes. Sometimes it is, yeah.

Andrew (*hoping this might be a bit of a revelation*) 'Sometimes it is'.

Isabella Yeah.

Andrew So it's possible that you could have been feeling tired on the day of the collision?

Isabella Um, I mean –

Andrew I'm saying it's possible? It's a *possibility*?

Isabella Yeah, well, I mean anything's possible.

Georgina Your Honour, Mr Eagleman is virtually *writing* my clients answers for her.

Jessup Is he?

Georgina In my opinion, Your Honour –

Jessup Your client's ability to remain alert strikes me as a vital element of this enquiry.

Georgina Your Honour, my client has admitted that she was at fault. That is not why we are here.

Jessup I see, yes. (*Beat.*) Mr Eagleman, if you have another line of enquiry that you wish to pursue, perhaps now would be a good point in the proceedings to do so.

Andrew In your statement, you claim that the collision took place at approximately three o'clock?

Isabella Yeah, it did.

Andrew Why are you so certain that it was three o'clock and not four o'clock, as Mr Needleman claims it was?

Isabella I finish at four on Mondays. As in, I have to be, like, clocked out *by* four. Like, at the latest.

Andrew What happens –   **Isabella** Also –

Isabella Sorry.

Andrew Please.

Isabella I still had a delivery.

Andrew You still had a delivery?

Isabella Yeah, in the back of the van. My last delivery on a Monday is like always at three. Mean the reason I remember is because one of the crates fell over. When I braked.

Kevin begins to send a text message on his mobile telephone, seemingly unnoticed.

Andrew One of the crates fell over?

Isabella Yeah, when I braked.

Andrew You must've been going quite fast then?

Isabella The crates are pretty light.

Andrew But it's a detail you remember?

Isabella What d'you mean?

Andrew The crate, toppling over, it's a detail from the day that you remember?

Isabella Well, I mean sort of.

Andrew Do your crates topple over often?

Georgina Your Honour, this is a descending into a farce – 'Do your crates topple over often?' Your Honour, please.

Jessup I fear Miss Burns may have a point, Mr Eagleman. Let's see if we can't pick up the pace a little.

Andrew Your Honour, the toppling of the crate seems to me to be of particular significance.

Jessup How so, Mr Eagleman?

Andrew If Miss Reynolds' braking was severe enough to cause the toppling of a crate that was *full*, then it strikes me, Your Honour, that Miss Reynolds' vehicle must have been moving at a fairly significant speed?

Georgina Your Honour, Mr Eagleman makes an interesting point, but his line of questioning needs to support that. He cannot simply –

Andrew Similarly, Your Honour, the crate seems to be vital in establishing the exact time of day –

Jessup Alright, alright. Thank you Miss Burns, thank you Mr Eagleman.

Beat. Jessup flicks through his 'bundle'. Kevin finishes the text message and, after looking up, checking around the court, begins another. Again, seemingly unnoticed.

Mr Eagleman, I would like you to draw the issue of the toppling crate to a close, and then I would like you to continue.

Andrew (*meaning 'thank you'*) Your Honour. Miss Reynolds, in your statement you claim that the driver of the vehicle with which you collided was non-white?

Isabella Yeah, he was sort of Greek-looking.

Andrew He was 'sort of Greek-looking'?

Jessup notices that Kevin is sending a text message.

Isabella Yeah, I don't mean to sound weird or anything, but he was sort of, like, he was sort of *dark*-looking.

Andrew 'Dark-looking'?

Isabella Yeah, not like dark as in black, but, like, dark as in definitely not white. And he had a sort of Greeky-looking beard.

Andrew A beard?

Isabella Yeah, like a, like a thick, bushy, wiry, Greeky-looking beard.

Andrew I see.

Isabella And he didn't really say that much.

Andrew Who didn't?

Isabella The bloke who got out of the car. I got the impression his . . . Got the impression that English probably wasn't his first language.

Andrew You mention very little of this in your statement, Miss Reynolds?

Isabella Yeah, I know, I know. And I feel, right, I feel really bad about that. But.

Andrew Miss Reynolds?

Isabella (*beat, then*) I didn't wanna sound racist.

Andrew In your statement?

Isabella I just wasn't really sure what the right word was. For someone who looks sorta Greek but also looks pretty dark an' that.

Andrew What did you speak about? Once the two of you were out of your respective vehicles.

Isabella looks to Georgina briefly.

Andrew Miss Reynolds?

Isabella I was running . . . I *was* running late.

Isabella hesitates briefly.

Andrew Miss Reynolds.

Isabella I heard the crate. When it went over. I heard it and I thought . . . I like swore, and then I got out of the van. I looked at the front of the van, right, at the like bumper and it looked fine. And then I like . . . looked at the car. Looked at the back of it. And I gotta be honest, right . . . When this bearded, like, burly-looking bloke got out of the car – Because you hear about situations like this properly just kicking off. And he looked *hard* –

Jessup What on earth do you think you are doing?!

All are momentarily stunned. Kevin immediately puts his mobile telephone away.

Andrew (*meaning 'Is something the matter?'*) Your Honour?

Jessup Your client has been *texting*.

Kevin I was tryin'a turn it off.

Jessup No, you weren't. Don't you lie. You were not. I have been watching you. You have been *texting*. There is a sign on the door, Mr Needleman, which very politely asks that all mobile telephones be turned *off*. If the matter is urgent, then I would ask you to leave.

Kevin I'm sorry.

Jessup I should think that you are. Unbelievable.

Jessup glares at Kevin, beat.

Mr Eagleman.

Andrew Thank you, Your Honour. Miss Reynolds . . . we were . . . we were discussing your . . . discussion with the . . . gentleman driving the vehicle, the vehicle that you collided with.

Isabella (*beat*) I offered him some money.

Georgina reacts to this.

Andrew Why did you offer money?

Isabella Sorta just panicked.

Andrew What was the gentleman's response?

Isabella That was the thing, right: he didn't. Didn't say anything. Got the impression he couldn't. Just gave me a piece of paper with his insurance details on. (*Points briefly at Kevin.*) But it definitely wasn't him. And I swear to you, right, there definitely wasn't anybody else in the car.

Andrew How can you be certain?

Isabella I checked.

Isabella looks to Georgina briefly.

Andrew Miss Reynolds?

Isabella This is gonna sound worse than it is, than it was, right, but . . . I was in an accident a couple of years ago.

Georgina reacts. Andrew can't quite believe his luck.

Andrew An accident?

Isabella Yeah.

Andrew Did you admit liability?

Isabella I was asleep, yeah.

Andrew You were *asleep*?   **Georgina** Your Honour –

Isabella For, like, *two seconds*, I fell asleep for like *literally* –

Andrew Is that why you offered Mr Needleman a sum of money following your collision, because you knew immediately that you would have to accept liability?

Isabella What?

Andrew *Why* did you offer
Mr Needleman a settlement   **Isabella** It wasn't him.
following your collision?

Given that your employers are responsible for insuring all of their vehicles and all of their drivers, I find it odd that your first instinct would be to attempt to *pay* Mr Needleman off?

Isabella I just thought it would be quicker.

Isabella I didn't wanna lose my job!

Andrew Why were you concerned you might lose your job? Miss Reynolds?

Isabella There definitely wasn't anybody else in the car because the last time I was in an accident, there was a little kid in the car. He was fine, right, he was like *literally* fine.

Andrew Miss Reynolds –

Isabella But that's why I checked. Because I was worried. Because of last time. I'm telling you, the car was empty. And it definitely wasn't him. He was Greek. He was big and he had a beard and he was Greek. And I don't care if that makes me a racist.

Later that day. Andrew, Barry, Kevin, Georgina, Isabella, Attendant and Jessup. Georgina sips a little water and stands.

Georgina Your Honour should be in no doubt that this is an extremely complex and intricate case. A slippery snake, if you will. However, I would urge Your Honour to bear in mind a number of glaring inconsistencies on the part of the claimants. As a mother, I find it staggering that the Needlemans resisted treating their daughter's apparent injuries until a week after the collision. Similarly, Your Honour, the notion that neither Mr nor Mrs Needleman at any point *physically* comforted their daughter strikes me as palpably untrue. The claimants would ask us to believe that the delay in their daughter receiving treatment is due to the timing of the collision itself: one day before a prearranged family holiday that not all of the family would be attending. They would *also* ask us to believe that their apparently injured daughter was woken up the following day, and asked to ride a train from Luton to Weymouth, a journey of at least three hours, Your Honour, with a veritable smorgasbord of neck, back and head injuries. If my son were ill or indeed injured, Your Honour, I can assure you that hell and high water would not be able to put a stop to me dropping everything. None of this, however, is intended as a criticism of the Needlemans' love and care for their daughter. Rather, it is about the legitimacy of their claims. Neither Mr nor Mrs Needleman, for instance, seems to know the reason they were paying a visit to the Arndale Shopping Centre on the day of their collision. Likewise, there is a vast disparity between the whys and the wherefores of a family holiday that only two-thirds of the family seemed interested in attending. Would one's own family, no matter how distant a relative they may be, would one's own family, Your Honour, not accept a car accident as an unavoidable, extenuating circumstance? Would one's own family not forgive a last-minute cancellation in light of a car accident? I know I certainly would. This was a minor incident, a benign claim. Money for old rope. In short, Your Honour, I put it to you that neither Lucy nor Jennifer Needleman were present during the collision itself. What we have here, is yet another ordinary, humble, hard-working family unnaturally galvanised by the ever-growing, ever-parasitic culture of no-win-no-fee.

Georgina sits. Andrew stands, flips through his tatty notebook and readies himself to speak.

Andrew Your Honour, I feel nauseous. At a time of recession, when jobs are scarce, and good, honest, hard-working families like the Needlemans are having to make do, one of the biggest supermarket chains in the UK sees fit to take on a man, his wife and their four-year-old daughter? Your Honour: what on earth are they out to prove? Miss Burns would have you believe that my clients are opportunists. That they hatched a plan from the comfort of their living room. This could not be further from the truth. Kevin and Jennifer Needleman are committed, loving parents. Miss Burns asks us to view the Needlemans through a prism of misdirection. She asks us to perceive their make-do attitude as something unnaturally disingenuous. Simply put, Your Honour, this is nonsensical. If the Needlemans were lying, if they had actively chosen to collude with one another, would their stories not be airtight? Would they not have ironed out the creases? The fact that they haven't is a testament to nothing more than the fallibility of the human memory. The truth cannot be accurate, it cannot be consistent. The truth can only ever be unfinished, *unfurnished*, Your Honour. Why would the Needlemans wish to cling on to one of the most traumatic chapters in their lives? In order to move forward, they have simply tried to forget.

Andrew, hot and sweaty, loosens his tie a little and wipes his brow.

There is the question of the 'lost week'. Miss Burns would have us believe that the Needlemans used the seven days between their collision and their visit to the doctors to hatch some kind of dastardly insurance scam. Nonsense. This is simply a family that doesn't like to make a fuss. This is a family that put their commitment to their relatives ahead of their own well-being. This is not a family that dwells. This is not a family that *succumbs*. This is a family that *copes*. I put it to you, Your Honour, that despite their minor inconsistencies, despite their infinitesimal flaws, the Needlemans are entirely trustworthy.

Andrew sits.

Jessup Well. Miss Burns, Mr Eagleman, thank you very much. Thought-provoking indeed. Indeed, so much so that I found myself *transported* back to my time as a student, would you believe. McGhee versus the National Coal Board, no less. It was Lord Reid, I believe, who said in his closing address, 'It has often been said that the legal concept of causation is not based on logic or philosophy. It is based on the practical way in which a man's mind works in the everyday affairs of life.' Anyway: there we are. Anecdotal food for thought perhaps.

Jessup turns off his fan.

Attendant All rise.

All stand. Jessup nods and exits. All begin to gather their belongings, etc.

Kevin Is that it?

Barry There's still the verdict.

Kevin How long's that take?

Barry Not long.

Kevin D' we have to wait around here?

Barry (*perhaps hands Kevin a couple of quid*) Go and get something to drink if y'want. *Soft drink.* I'll give you a ring when they want us back. Don't go too far.

Kevin (*to Andrew*) Mate: that was fucking great. I'm serious.

Exit Kevin.

Georgina Well done, you.

Andrew spins around to face Georgina.

Andrew Likewise.

Exit Georgina and Isabella.

Andrew What d'ya reckon?

Barry 'Bout what?

Andrew All that. How'd we do? Honest opinion.

Barry We lied, Andrew. That's all we did. Let's go and get a bit of fresh air.

Andrew I'm alright.

Barry How about a drink?

Andrew I'm alright.

Barry Horse tranquilliser?

Beat.

Andrew Think I'm just gonna hang on here.

Beat.

Barry I'm on the mobile if you need anything.

Exit Barry. Andrew sits, alone.

Three

Autumn. Scorpion Claims. Day. The office is bare except for a number of brown, removal-type cardboard boxes. Outside it is raining heavily. Barry and Kevin. Barry is dressed casually. Kevin is wearing both a brand-new black-leather jacket (a touch too big for him perhaps) and a fairly elaborate pair of box-fresh trainers, Nike for instance. He also perhaps now wears several new gold rings. He is holding an unopened bottle of Louis Roederer Cristal champagne. Also, there is a white, cardboard cake box. Mid-conversation:

Kevin Couldn't believe it when he caught me texting. Went fucking ballistic, didn't he? Thought I'd fucked it. Thought I'd proper fucked it. 'Didn't you see the sign on the fucking door?' Nearly shit m'self. 'Kin Andrew, though. That fucking speech. Mean, I was fucking wellin' up! (*Beat.*) He ever tell ya what happened at his last place?

Barry How d'ya mean?

Kevin I heard he got the sack.

Barry Who told y' that?

Kevin A little bird who prowls the streets of Luton looking for top-notch gossip.

Barry Y'd have t' ask the man himself.

Kevin Can't believe y' calling it a day. We was on a roll, Barry. We had people queuing up 'round the fucking block.

Barry Did we?

Kevin People were Facebooking me saying, alright mate, long-time-no-see, hear y'got a little business going?

Barry (*beat: 'penny drops'*) Right.

Kevin I was up for, fucking, pyramids, fucking, triangles, whatever y' call em – You know, them catalogues y' get through y'door – Hoovers and shit. Reckon we coulda done one o' those f' no-win-no-fees. End up like Theo whatshisname, Ryman's an' that?

Barry Paphitis.

Kevin Paphitis. 'You want me to give you ten thousand pounds of my children's inheritance?' Sky's the limit, Bazza. Still could be. Savvy move, closing this place. Chance to rebrand.

Barry Ah, look, ya know I'd love to. But I'm moving.

Kevin So I gather, Bazza. Remind me again where'bouts?

Barry Up north.

Kevin Whippets and shit is it?

Barry ?

Kevin Sure we can't convince y'ta stay down *sowf*? 'S after all where the money is at.

Barry Family, innit.

Kevin Is it?

Barry Yeah, m'daughter –

Kevin Thass right, thass right, course it is. How's she getting on?

Barry Yeah, good.

Kevin Remind me why she's ended up in the arse-end of nowhere again?

Barry Student. Doin' a degree.

Kevin Thass right, thass right. Fuckin' brain-box; takes after her old man, naturally. An' how's she getting on with that, whatd'yacallit, spinal some'in-or-other?

Barry How many o' them claims you reckon we put through in the end, Kevin?

Kevin All in?

Barry All in.

Kevin Fuck knows, mate. Lost count! Fifty? Sixty?

Barry Unbelievable, innit. What we managed to get away with.

Kevin Mate: tell me about it. We're like the fucking Lemur Brothers o' Luton.

Beat, then:

Fuck it; why don't we just open it now? (*Of the Cristal.*) 'S good shit this. Y' ever had it?

Barry Can't say that I have.

Kevin Five hundred quid a bottle. Puff Daddy and that lot rave about it.

Barry ?

Kevin Daddy. Puff Daddy. He's a rapper.

Barry Must be doing alright for himself.

Kevin (*not a Puff Daddy song, but sung pretty well nonetheless*) 'He give me money, when I'm in n-e-e-d. Go 'head girl, go 'head get down.'

Barry Not ringing any bells, I'm afraid.

Kevin Fair enough.

Enter Andrew, wet, with a broken umbrella and a bag containing a Chinese takeaway. He is dressed casually.

Here he is, look. Speak of the devil. Bit wet?

Andrew (*beat*) This is a surprise.

Barry Kevin's brought us a bottle of champers.

Kevin Cristal.

Barry Kevin's brought us a bottle of Cristal.

Kevin Five hundred quid a bottle.

Andrew Right.

Kevin You alright? Look like y'seen a ghost?

No response.

(*Cristal.*) What d'ya say? Fancy a little go on the ol' (*As in the song.*) 'Louis Louis'?

Andrew I'm alright actually, Kevin.

Kevin begins to unwrap the Cristal.

Kevin Saw this bloke on telly, 'Gyptian or something, opened it with a fucking sword. Pulls it out of his fucking holster whatever 's called, and just fucking –

He gestures, demonstrates.

Andrew I'm alright actually, Kevin.

Kevin Trust me: this is gonna blow y' fucking mind.

Andrew I'm alright.

Kevin continues to prepare the Cristal for opening. Andrew snatches the Cristal from Kevin.

Kevin 'Oah – Fuck d'ya   **Andrew** We're alright.
think y'doing?

Andrew 'S the middle of the day.

Beat.

Barry Kevin, mate, thanks for popping down –

Kevin Whoa, no, hold on. Hold on. Not just here bearing gifts. Got a proposition for ya. Wondered if y' fancied giving it another go? 'Where there's blame there's a claim.'

Andrew Is this a joke?

Kevin We're a team now, baby. Christ, 's like a proper fucking morgue in here.

Barry Thanks for coming down, Kevin.

Kevin Least have a fucking think about it.

Andrew No.

Kevin It speaks.

Barry Alright –

Kevin I'm just tryin'a drum up a bit of business for ya, mate. Y' as bad as Jen. Fucking moaning about this, moaning about that. Right fucking sourpuss. Come on, Andy, stop acting like a fucking bitch and just say 'yes' will ya?

Andrew What did you say?

Kevin Maybe we should have another chat when y' not looking quite s' fucking *wet*.

Andrew goes for Kevin, charges toward him – Andrew grabs Kevin and Kevin grabs Andrew – Andrew shoves Kevin against the wall, hard, and Kevin registers the pain – Kevin headbutts Andrew. Andrew loses his grip on Kevin as he lifts a hand to his own nose. Andrew swings for Kevin suddenly, hitting him in the face, Barry reacts, moving forward (perhaps uttering the odd 'Okay' etc.), Kevin grabs Andrew around the waist and the pair clatter on to the floor, perhaps tumbling into some of the brown removal-type cardboard boxes. Kevin is now on top of Andrew and lands a fist to Andrew's face. Barry tries to pull Kevin away from Andrew. Kevin, however, manages to catch Barry in

the face with his elbow as he goes to land his second
punch to Andrew's face. As Kevin turns slightly to see
what has happened to Barry, Andrew grabs hold of
Kevin's head and smacks it against the floor – again,
the pain registers acutely on Kevin's face. Andrew now
kneels above Kevin and hits him again and again and
again, Kevin's head slowly becoming more and more
lifeless. Finally, Barry moves to Andrew and, with a
great deal of effort, lifts Andrew away from Kevin
extremely clumsily. To a greater or lesser degree, this
should all happen incredibly quickly and should be
visceral and messy and feral. Beat. Kevin is crying,
weeping, very quietly, trying to catch his breath. Barry
moves to Kevin and attempts to inspect Kevin's bloody
face. Kevin jerks away.

Barry Need to stay still. Kevin, listen to me, need ya
t' try and stay still –

Kevin (*perhaps not entirely audible*) My fucking face.

Exit Barry. Silence except for the breathing and/or
weeping of Kevin and Andrew. Enter Barry with a
bowl of water and a J-cloth. Barry moves to Kevin and
begins to clean the blood away from Kevin's face.

Barry We're gonna need to take ya t' A&E. Alright?
Think y'nose might be broken.

Kevin I'm gonna fucking sue you, I am gonna fucking
SUE YOU.

Andrew I'm a fucking solicitor!

Beat. Kevin tries to stand suddenly.

Barry Kevin, y'need to stay still, mate, needya t'try and stay still.	**Kevin** (*perhaps not entirely audible*) Don't fucking touch me, don't fucking touch me.

Kevin is on his feet. Kevin moves through the room, picks up the bottle of Cristal and stops. Kevin spits blood on the floor; not necessarily at Andrew, but rather just to clear the blood from his mouth.

Kevin Don't think y'better than me.

Exit Kevin. Barry watches Andrew, beat. Barry moves to Andrew and inspects his hands, his knuckles.

Barry Musta hit his teeth.

Andrew 'S fine.

Barry Might need stitches.

Andrew I'm fine.

Beat.

Barry (*takeaway*) What'd'ya get?

Andrew Set meal for two.

Barry Oh yeah.

Andrew Yeah. Special fried rice.

Barry Oh yeah.

Andrew Yeah. Beef chop suey.

Barry Nice.

Andrew Sweet and sour chicken balls.

Barry Love a good ball. How many d'ya get?

Andrew Twelve.

Barry Nice.

Andrew And then a coupla pancake rolls. Make 'em themselves.

Barry Oh yeah.

Andrew Yeah.

Barry Job done.

Beat.

Andrew Whass in the box?

Barry Dunno.

Andrew moves to the cake box and lifts the lid.

Andrew Fuck's sake.

Barry What?

Barry moves to the cake and looks.

What is it?

Andrew 'S a scorpion.

Barry Y' shouldn'ta lied.

Andrew What?

Barry To me.

Andrew Dunno what y' talking about.

Barry Yes you do. I asked you. I asked you, Andrew.

Andrew I didn't lie t' ya, Barry.

Beat.

Barry Better clear all this up.

Using the cloth and the bowl of water, Barry cleans up any blood that is on the floor. Andrew watches.

Andrew D'you wanna hand?

Barry doesn't respond. Finished, Barry takes the cloth and the bloody bowl of water, and exits.

Later that day. Scorpion Claims. It is still raining. Andrew and Jennifer. Jennifer wears a large, puffy, synthetic coat.

Andrew Y've lost y'bump?

Jennifer I've what?

Andrew Y'bump, 's gone.

Jennifer You mean my baby?

Andrew Yeah.

Jennifer You mean I've given birth since you last saw me?

Andrew Yeah.

Jennifer No wonder y'such a good solicitor; you do not miss a thing, Andrew Eagleman.

Andrew How'd it go?

Jennifer Felt like I was tryin'a shit out a watermelon.

Andrew Right.

Jennifer For ten hours.

Andrew Boy or girl?

Jennifer Girl. Aslan.

Andrew Come again?

Jennifer Aslan. Midwife thought it was a bit much, but I'm really glad we stuck to our guns.

Andrew . . .

Jennifer Her name's Heather. I was really sorry t' hear about y' dad, Andrew. (*Beat.*) Are you alright?

Andrew He only really managed a headbutt.

Jennifer I wasn't talking about the fight.

Andrew How's his nose?

Jennifer Broken.

Andrew Shit, really?

Jennifer Looks like Hannibal Lecter.

Andrew Shit. I'm sorry.

Jennifer No y' not.

Andrew Y' right; I'm not.

Jennifer Says he's gonna sue ya.

Andrew Good luck to him.

Jennifer Thinking of going to m' sister's.

Andrew Right.

Jennifer Stay with her for a bit.

Andrew Why's that?

Jennifer Take the kids.

Andrew Everything alright?

Beat.

Why the fuck d'ya marry him, Jen?

Jennifer gasps/snorts/laughs, taken aback.

Jennifer Sort of a question's that?

Andrew He's a fucking arsehole.

Jennifer Yeah. Well. Takes one to know one, doesn't it?

Andrew When I heard you two were together, I was fucking gutted.

Jennifer What on earth is that supposed to mean?

Andrew For you. I was fucking gutted for you.

Jennifer That's because you're a snob.

Andrew Just never imagined you'd end up . . .

Jennifer What?

Andrew Doesn't matter.

Jennifer No, go on, what? You never imagined I'd end up what?

Andrew Working in M&S with two fucking kids.

Jennifer Fuck's that supposed to mean?

Andrew You coulda done anything.

Jennifer I *wanted* to have children, Andrew.

Andrew Did you?

Jennifer Reckon you must be in shock or something.

Andrew You wanted kids, or you wanted kids with him?

Jennifer Both.

Andrew Bullshit.

Jennifer You should know.

Andrew Meaning what?

Jennifer Meaning least I'm not the one who makes a livin' out of it.

Andrew Kids?

Jennifer 'Bullshit'.

Andrew Change the record.

Jennifer I would but there aren't any other records.

Andrew What does that even mean?

Jennifer I don't know, but it sounded clever so I said it. Why did you wanna see me?

Andrew What?

Jennifer Why did *you* want to see *me*?

Andrew I didn't.

Jennifer What?

Andrew Barry said you wanted to see me.

Jennifer He said to me you wanted to see me.

Andrew Fuck's sake.

Beat.

I get it in the neck all the time, you know. That *tone*, that look; whenever someone asks me what I do and I say I'm a solicitor and they say what area and I say personal injury. They look at me as if I'm the one with the problem. But you wanna know what the real problem is?

Jennifer Not particularly.

Andrew 'S people like Kevin. People whose lives're so fucking devoid of meaning, they end up tryin' a fill their houses with a loada' shit they don't even fucking *need*, let alone want, and all because they wanna feel *significant*. Fucking TVs and trainers and fucking five hundred quid bottles o' champagne. And the worse thing is: it isn't even their fault. Because 's everywhere.

Jennifer Our lives have plenty of meaning, actually. Least we didn't leave and get dragged back and end up hating ourselves for it. I like it here. I like the people.

Andrew Minute ago you said you were fucking leaving?

Jennifer Oh, fuck off back to London.

Beat.

Andrew Where's y' sister live? (*Beat.*) Jen –

Jennifer Southampton.

Andrew How long y' thinking of goin' for? (*Beat.*) Jen, how long y' thinking –

Jennifer Dunno.

Beat.

Andrew I'm sorry.

Jennifer No y' not.

Andrew I am. Look at me.

Beat.

Jennifer What y' gonna do now?

Andrew How d'ya mean?

Jennifer Now this place is no more.

Andrew Dunno.

Jennifer What d'ya wanna do?

Andrew Dunno.

Beat.

When I was four, I trod on this nail. Went straight through my foot. Screamed, started crying, top of my voice. Dad came rushing out, came charging up to me. He picked me up and he wrapped a navy-blue scarf around my foot. Kept screaming, crying, whole street could hear. Then he says, 'Look at me.' 'Look at me,' he says. So I did, I looked at him. I looked him right in the eyes. And I stopped crying.

Jennifer moves to Andrew, very close. The sound of the rain outside fills the room.